◆◇◆ PERCEPTIONS IN
PUBLIC HIGHER EDUCATION

PERCEPTIONS IN PUBLIC HIGHER EDUCATION

Edited by

Gene A. Budig

UNIVERSITY OF NEBRASKA PRESS • LINCOLN

Publishers on the Plains

UNP

Copyright © 1970 by the University of Nebraska Press

All rights reserved

Standard Book Number 8032-0749-2

Library of Congress Catalog Card Number 71-05647

Manufactured in the United States of America

CONTENTS

FOREWORD

◆◇◆ IN MANY RESPECTS the American public university of today is a unique organization. Its mixed heritage has produced an interesting blend of the British traditions in undergraduate education, the German concepts of graduate study and research, and the uniquely American dedication to serving its public constituency. Even in the face of current confrontation and challenge from elements of the student body, the widespread public acceptance and support of its programs represent eloquent testimony to its many successes.

The concepts of a university's organization are firmly rooted in the pages of history. Its task, as Alfred North Whitehead suggested, "is the creation of the future as far as rational thought and civilized modes of appreciation can affect the issue." Out of the ebb and flow of the political tides in Western civilization have evolved the traditions and the organization of the institutions where rational thought and civilized modes of appreciation can flourish. It has been designed to insulate the individual professor from the external pressures of the moment which might dictate what and how he teaches in his quest for truth. Within his own classroom the professor has virtually complete autonomy, and the academic organization of which he is such a vital part is designed to preserve his independence of thought and action. It is his success with the individual student, endowed with a formidable spectrum of talents and interests, to which the academic enterprise is dedicated. Yet the sheer magnitude of the operation in the multi-purpose university of today demands management and business practices as responsive as the latest generation of computers will permit.

The basic functions of the university in disseminating, applying, and expanding man's fund of knowledge rest with the faculty composed of individual professionals grouped in a somewhat arbitrary way into college faculties with authority for virtually all phases of the academic program, including the requirements for admission, course of study, and the determination of those who complete the program.

The multi-college university has traditionally delegated additional authority to the faculty-as-a-whole in matters which transcend the disciplines defined by a college designation. The result is a diffusion of the decision-making process which defies the logic of the traditional business organization and is a source of complete bewilderment to the layman.

The quality of a university becomes the summation of the competence and the productivity of its faculty members who individually and collectively make the innumerable decisions which determine the outcome of the university's primary mission. What, then, is the role of administrators and administration? There is a strong element of service in providing the environment and the resources conducive for faculty productivity. In a very real sense, administration provides logistical support and those essential services which will free the faculty for creative effort in teaching and research. The administrator's role includes establishing and maintaining the mechanisms for the interchange of information and ideas among all elements of the academic community as a fundamental part of the decision-making process. This is not to deny the administrator his traditional role of leadership, but as a leader he must successfully use his powers of suggestion, logic, persuasion, and influence rather than the autocratic prerogatives of office.

It would seem that the typical pyramid, symbolic of most organizational structures, is quite inadequate for representation of the decision-making process within a university. It is accurate enough for some of the functions of management, such as the allocation of resources and the priority judgments which influence the general direction of the institutional effort. But a more complete view of university administration must recognize the presence of an inverted pyramid where the broad base controls the vital decisions which determine the relative success of the educational enterprise. Recommendations for faculty appointment and for distribution of the rewards and emoluments to the faculty initiate from that broad base, and the administrative hierarchy exerts influence by reaction rather than initiative.

The success of a chief executive officer is often measured by his ability to attract the financial resources for the educational enterprise. For the public institution, public confidence and understanding, as well as credibility, become the essential ingredients for support. All of these can be profoundly influenced by the public behavior and attitudes of students, faculty, administrators, and the governing board—factors over which he has little control. But academic administrators can falter within the institution without a continuing awareness of the limitations of office in directing the academic effort of the faculty. There is a delicate balance between administrative initiative and judgments tempered by faculty counsel. It is small wonder, therefore, that a chief executive's tenure in office is relatively brief.

Clifford Morris Hardin, who guided the destinies of the University of Nebraska for more than fourteen years and who now serves as United States Secretary of Agriculture, provides one of the exceptions to this generalization. To some degree his example has influenced all of the contributors to this collection of essays.

MERK HOBSON
Acting Chancellor
University of Nebraska

◆◇◆◇◆◇◆◇◆◇◆

INTRODUCTION

◆◇◆ NEVER HAS THE MAN ON THE STREET expected more
from public higher education than he does today. In a
very real sense, he expects our colleges and universities
to answer many of the unanswerable questions of our
time. As Lyndon Baines Johnson observed: "We expect
the institutions of higher learning to right many of
society's wrongs such as poverty and racial injustice; we
expect them to make the lame walk and to devise ways
to feed the world's hungry; and we expect them to offer
blueprints for the immediate curbing of inflation."

The expectations are both impressive and flattering,
but at the same time ironic when one considers that
never has that same man on the street been more appre-
hensive about our colleges and universities than he is
today. National opinion surveys, including those of
Gallup and Harris, indicate that the great preponder-
ance of American citizens are "visibly uneasy" about the
educational community and its extracurricular activities
in recent years. That uneasiness has had an adverse

effect on the public's willingness to support the programs of public higher education; in some instances the very basis of academic freedom has been questioned. Many politicians have found it popular to deface academia with accusations and threats. There has been a rash of punitive and restrictive legislative measures introduced around the country. A number of them have become law. Campus disruptions, in some instances, have impaired major institutional programs to the extent that needed financial support and public favor have been withheld.

Those of us associated with higher education must become more concerned about interpreting our institutions' objectives, responsibilities, and activities to the public. We have been complacent for too long. We must, as Robert Goheen suggests, participate in a crusade to educate not only the general public, but also many of our students, faculty members, and administrators about the ways and means of our colleges and universities. With this volume of essays the University of Nebraska joins that worthy educational crusade.

We did not set out to serve the young administrator in higher learning with a master plan for his professional growth. The contrary was true. The essays were structured to raise philosophical questions, to stir creative answers, and, as the title indicates, to offer perceptions in public higher education. The contributors to this volume are men of experience, integrity, and imagination. They are all dedicated to the shaping and expediting of educational policy that will enhance the public well-being. Their essays are written to increase public understanding and trust in the institutions of higher education; their essays represent an attempt to enlarge the meaningful literature on higher education.

We believe the volume is unique in that it brings together the observations of a group of individuals engaged in the awesome and yet stimulating task of directing the progress of a single major public university. Although in some ways a composite, the essays clearly illustrate the divergence of opinion that can be found on a given campus. They forcefully emphasize the importance and role of divergence within the academy. As David Henry once said: "The strength of a great university is in its depth and divergency."

By this measure the University of Nebraska has a strong and vibrant fiber; it is, in many ways, representative of other progressive institutions of public higher learning.

GENE A. BUDIG

THE CAMPUS PRESIDENCY

Joseph Soshnik

◆◇◆ THESE ARE TIMES when authors seem to move easily and frequently from one psychological, sociological, or cultural phenomenon to another. Without question college and university issues and figures are in vogue these days as subjects for inquiry, evaluation, debate, and pronouncement. It is not surprising that the college and university administrator has himself been brought under the microscope with increasing frequency.

In a sense, it is flattering to read and hear thousands of words about one's calling. There is a type of psychological lift in being at the center of both professional and lay interest. There is a hard-to-describe sensation in finding oneself in the position of simultaneously looking into the microscope and being the specimen on the slide.

This essay is not an all-encompassing commentary on the campus presidency. It is a series of observations offered by a "new president," who considers himself to be an old-timer in higher education. The following paragraphs will deal not only with the conventional enumeration of areas of responsibility, but perhaps more significantly with a new president's sense of the unique or special role of the presidency within the institution.

Formal definitions and distinctions would lead to differentiation of institutions and presidential roles in terms of institutional control classification (private or public), institutional size, the ages or traditions of the institutions, etc. This essay will not offer formal distinctions; it begins with an acknowledgment that, among other differences, presidential roles will vary significantly in terms of balance between "internal" and "external" responsibilities.

Increasing attention is being given to the possibility of increased "division of labor" between two central administrators. Titles are not used with complete uniformity, but typically the position designations are "chancellor" and "president." One of the administrators, under such an arrangement, would assume primary responsibility for external relationships: legislative relations (for publicly controlled institutions), alumni relations, relationships with foundations and other donors, etc. The other administrator, with considerably reduced responsibility for external affairs, would be designated as the chief administrator for the internal affairs of the institution.

As state universities have grown and added new campuses, the division-of-labor concept has led to an arrangement similar to the one just noted. In these instances, one administrator (chancellor or president, depending upon local usage) serves as the chief executive officer for the governing board. His primary duties are to work with the board in the external relationships of the institution (especially legislative relations) and to provide leadership and coordination for the component campuses of the total university. The second "central" administrator is assigned responsibility for internal affairs.

The remainder of this essay will deal with those aspects of the presidency which, for the most part, may be labeled "internal."

The President and His Responsibilities

Functions and responsibilities of chief executives have been treated extensively in the literature of management. The more specialized literature dealing with college and university administration, with varying emphases and viewpoints, provides an increasingly stereotyped outline of presidential responsibilities—largely in terms of on-campus constituencies. As noted earlier, detailed job descriptions for a college or university presidency—in real-life situations—are influenced greatly by local circumstances. Nevertheless, all college and university presidents are called upon to plan, organize, staff, direct, coordinate, report, and budget ("POSDCORB," as outlined by Gulick and Urwick).[1] Louis Benezet has said that "the presiding function can be divided into three parts: organizing and advancing, operating, and

---

1. Luther H. Gulick and L. Urwick, *Papers on the Science of Administration* (New York: Institute of Public Administration, Columbia University, 1937), p. 13.

preserving." [2] Benezet also pointed out: "Some presidents are especially good at organizing and advancing, others at operating, and still others, particularly the old hands, at preserving. But there is no truly successful president who sooner or later does not achieve mastery over all of them." [3]

In a major study published in 1967, Demerath, Stephens, and Taylor included the following paragraph:

> Asked for his opinion of the new president of his university, a professor said, "I don't know anything about him, but I hope he has enough sense to leave the faculty alone." We do not know how widespread this attitude is, but the statement points up two basic aspects of the university presidency: extensive delegation of responsibility for educational management, and effective tenure by faculty sufferance. [4]

With rare but significant exceptions, the president's role in academic administration is essentially a supportive role. Later in this essay attention will be given to certain unique contributions of the president that go beyond mere support. As regards day-to-day, recurring academic administration, however, most campuses dis-

---

2. Gerald P. Burns, *Administrators in Higher Education: Their Functions and Coordination* (New York: Harper & Brothers, 1962), p. 101.

3. Ibid.

4. Nicholas J. Demerath, Robert W. Stephens, and R. Robb Taylor, *Power, Presidents, and Professors* (New York: Basic Books, Inc., 1967), p. 79.

close a pattern of very considerable decentralization. Individual academic departments, and to some extent interdepartmental or collegiate committees, are responsible for the bulk of the decisions made with respect to curricular matters. Faculty groups of varying nature, through traditional delegations of authority and responsibility, also establish grading systems, academic calendars, requirements for special honors, etc. Only when questions of finance, organizational jurisdiction, or compatibility with broad institutional policy arise do these subjects become matters of direct presidential involvement.

The president's influence in academic affairs—typically in concert with the dean of faculties—comes most frequently in personnel matters. The president and dean of faculties—after considerable discussion with collegiate deans and other academic administrators—enunciate broad standards and guides intended to govern decisions with respect to selection of new faculty, promotion and tenure, compensation, etc.

Active participation by the president and dean of faculties in interviewing faculty prospects provides opportunity to help shape the academic endeavors of the institution. The principal contribution of the central administrators in such interviews frequently is not so much involved in evaluating the prospect as in convincing the prospect of the desirability and future promise of the institution. A side benefit of such interviews is that the department chairman, who accompanies the prospect, usually adds to the knowledge and awareness of the president (and often the dean of faculties) of programs, objectives, and aspirations of the department itself. In a very real sense these interviews constitute an important "tool of the trade" for the president.

Although financial administration is identified here as a role separate from academic administration, the two presidential roles—academic and financial—are tied *inextricably* together. All other considerations aside, allocation of financial resources is a dominant consideration in the strength and well-being of academic departments and programs.

The influence or accomplishments of the president in academic affairs, or the lack of them, can be measured only over long periods of time. In financial affairs, measurement and evaluation are frequently tied to precise fiscal periods and often made in terms of widely accepted standards. It is, of course, a truism that the level of external support influences greatly the program accomplishments of the institution. Given the finite bounds of resources available during a specified period of time, however, the president's role may then best be identified as one of establishing goals and priorities and of making corresponding internal allocation of resources. In this role the president must look to deans, chairmen, and other administrators for recommendations and proposals. Far more than in the academic affairs area, however, the president will apply direct managerial planning and control measures.

Budget making and financial reporting for colleges and universities have become more sophisticated and meaningful in recent years. Effective use of computers and computerized procedures in financial administration provide the president, central business and finance officers, and other university administrators vastly improved means for successful financial planning and control.

A major responsibility of the president, working closely with the institution's chief financial administrator, is to insure that financial procedures are used constructively. Deviousness, secrecy, and mystery are not devices peculiar to any single professional group on the college or university campus. Earlier suspicions and conflicts between academic and financial administrators stemmed largely from application of the "mystification principle" on both sides. The president's contribution in the business and finance area, simply stated, is one of leadership. It is his responsibility to insure that business and finance staff recognize their supportive or staff roles in the endeavors of the institution. Business and finance functions, the president must make clear, are not ends in themselves. At the same time, he must insure that the academic community understands the importance of properly designed business and finance procedures. Dissipation of resources or violation of legal requirements, he and other administrators must make clear, are destructive of the well-being of the academic entities themselves.

Despite the increasingly diverse responsibilities carried by our colleges and universities in recent years, it is felt by an overwhelming proportion of the general population (and by most members of the academic community) that teaching remains the institutions' central and most important responsibility. The complexity of student relations is the inevitable consequence of the greatly varied characteristics and the steadily increasing numbers of students who come—or who are sent—to college and university campuses. The decade of the sixties has been a decade in which issues and problems of our total society have become major "on-campus" concerns. The energy, compassion, and widespread idealism of America's young adults have caused unprecedented activism—most frequently orderly but on occasion disruptive—on college and university campuses. The broad and deep social issues of our times have, it seems, become catalysts for student concern and involvement within their campus environment. Differences in viewpoint, judgment, and in at least some instances values, have made college and university campus environments evermore volatile.

This essay will not attempt to explore specific issues of student concern, nor will it offer blueprints for campus organization and procedure in the area of student relations. The reality of intensified student interest and involvement, however, is a consideration of utmost importance in any examination of college and university organization, policies, and practices.

Although college and university presidents are not *ipso facto* student affairs specialists, they must necessarily

—given the fact of existing student concerns—become personally involved in programs, activities, and discussions deemed by students to be of significant concern within the institution. Reflection will quickly alert any observer to the paradoxes in arguments or assertions in favor of presidential participation in an infinite array of on-campus student activities. Nevertheless, any indication by the president of either disinterest or disdain will have an electrifying effect on a significant part of his student constituency. Among the "internal" concerns of students is a mounting conviction that students—and the teaching and other services toward the costs of which tuition and fee revenues are applied—are considered by faculty and administrators to be less important than other institutional or personal objectives: research, consultation, national prestige, etc. Though largely unwarranted and often overdrawn, these concerns—and the vital importance of removing any legitimate causes for the concerns—must be recognized by the president as he assigns priorities to his own activities.

The growth in numbers and ever-increasing importance of competent student personnel specialists is well known to all informed observers in higher education. No less than with his dean of faculties and with his director of business and finance, the president must maintain with the dean of student affairs close and unbroken contact. Furthermore, in common with the academic affairs area, student affairs programs will be effective or ineffective—in large degree—in direct relation to the willingness of the president to allocate financial resources to their support.

The president—with the direct participation of the dean of faculties, other academic administrators, and influential faculty members—can make perhaps his most important contribution toward effective student relations by means of one important and continuing effort: very extensive involvement of the faculty in student affairs. Faculty relationships with students, both in and out of the classroom, hardly need cataloguing here. Despite the obviousness of the key role of faculty members in the education and personal development of students, much needs to be done on many campuses to insure that this role can be performed effectively. If, in fact, "remoteness" and "impersonality" are legitimate concerns on some campuses, such complaints cannot be overcome through intensified and enlarged contacts with students on the part of the president and the dean of students alone. The president's role, once again, is one of leadership. The president and his associates in academic affairs must recruit, encourage, and reward faculty members who—in keeping with the best traditions of their profession—accept willingly the responsibilities of good teaching and effective counseling.

Balancing and Interpreting Aims

Up to this point, with only limited exception, the role of the president has been examined largely in terms of separate managerial or constituency functions. The usefulness of such an approach, in the interest of diagnosis and classification, is of course apparent. Nevertheless, the limitation of this approach is that it emphasizes parts rather than the whole. Although compartmentalization of the presidential role is useful for purposes of analysis, tendencies in "real life" to compartmentalize the president's efforts would have deleterious reactions upon his effectiveness.

Despite their unique characteristics, colleges and universities have many features in common with other man-made institutions. Colleges, departments, and other organizational entities within a university may be likened to "departments" established along product, functional, or geographic lines. Interrelationships, cooperation, and competition among these "departments" are both inherent and contrived. Cooperation, competition—and controversy—are the by-products of departmental aims and objectives, and of the professionalism, predilections, and prejudices of the "real-life" specialized personnel who staff and administer these departments. Reference was made earlier to conflicts between academic and financial administrators. (During World War II an Australian army officer was heard to refer to "the tyranny of the ancillary personnel.") Interdepartmental conflict is by no means limited, however, to differences between "line" departments on the one hand and "staff" departments on the other. Jurisdictional and philosophical disputes between and among academic departments are by no means unknown on college and university campuses. Given a chronic situation of "scarcity of resources," moreover, interdepartmental competition for funds at budget time is in effect a "way of life" on the campus.

A further complication for the president and his advisers is that external influences may intermittently disrupt internal planning and carefully established balances among departments. The impact of earmarked legislative appropriations is well understood and needs no elaboration. Other external influences can also lead, if not carefully evaluated, to "have" and "have not" situations among colleges and departments within the university.

Especially significant in recent years, as external influences on the potential for "imbalance" within institutions, have been federal government, foundation, and other project grants and contracts. Among the more recent variations have been "development" and "special improvement" grants, which provide outside funds for limited periods of time (typically three to five years). By the end of the grant period it is assumed the institution will have developed sufficient local resources to replace the outside resources no longer available by reason of grant expiration. In the face of the "chronic scarcity of resources," outside funds have great allure. The president and his advisers are urged by faculty and other staff to authorize acceptance of such outside financial support. In some quarters—including the granting agencies themselves—the volume of grant and contract awards received by the institution is considered to be an index of the institution's quality.

Clearly, the responsibility of the president is to maintain a global view as he gives consideration to the multiplicity of proposals from many parts of the institution. Inevitably, in any organization, some administrators will be more energetic, imaginative, or persuasive than others. Despite some urging to do so, the president must not accept the survival-of-the-fittest proposition. He, perhaps more than anyone else on the campus, *must* insist that appropriate balance be maintained in the development of institutional programs.

It is probably self-evident that the "global view" obligation of the president prevails also when he represents his institution to the governing board, legislature, and outside publics. A sizeable catalogue might be developed of potential requests, proposals, criticisms, complaints, and demands that might be presented by persons or groups outside the institution. Although there is no uniformity as to how the outside world communicates with the university, the president becomes involved—through either external or internal request—whenever a significant issue of policy or institutional philosophy is involved.

On occasion, when outside complaints are heard—especially where faculty and student views and utterances are involved—the president is called upon to defend faculty and student citizenship rights (including freedom of speech) even though the views expressed are completely contrary to his own. The college or university president—and an overwhelming proportion of his colleagues on the campus—recognize the responsibilities imposed by the freedom of thought and inquiry granted to the academic community. Fortunately, the traditions of the academic community and the high professional ideals which prevail lead to responsible conduct with only rare violations of the restraints of law or good taste. On those rare occasions, however, the president—as the interpreter to the public of the aims of education—is called upon to defend, not illegal or immoral acts, but freedom of inquiry and freedom of expression. In this arena, the chief executive of a college or university—despite many similarities in function to his counterparts in business and industry—has a unique executive role.

Above all other considerations, the president must be clear in his own appraisals of the institution he serves, and he must be consistent as he guides it. As he initiates activities and as he responds to proposals brought to him, he must measure, interpret, and evaluate specific actions in terms of institutional aims and objectives. Though advised and aided by many persons, he is the primary guardian of the central mission and long-term good health of a total educational community.

◆◇◆ **Supplementary Readings** ◆◇◆

Harold W. Dodds. *The Academic President—Educator or Caretaker?* New York: McGraw-Hill Book Company, 1962.

Clark Kerr. *The Uses of the University.* Cambridge: Harvard University Press, 1963.

Ralph Prator. *The College President.* New York: Center for Applied Research in Education, Inc., 1963.

Francis E. Rourke and Glenn E. Brooks. *The Managerial Revolution in Higher Education.* Baltimore: The Johns Hopkins Press, 1966.

Harold W. Stoke. *The American College President.* New York: Harper and Bros., 1959.

Henry M. Wriston. *Academic Procession, Reflections of a College President.* New York: Columbia University Press, 1959.

THE DEAN OF FACULTIES

C. Peter Magrath

◆◇◆ IN A LARGE, MULTIPURPOSE (or multiproblem) university, the dean of faculties must be a multipurpose man. His precise concerns and functions will naturally differ from university to university. Organizational patterns, administrative and faculty personalities, and the personal style of the deans themselves will almost certainly vary. Since each university is a somewhat individual administrative and political system, no two deans of faculties will ever be quite alike in functions and responsibilities.

There is, then, no dean of faculties handbook to describe and prescribe for all who hold that assignment, which is labeled a vice presidency for academic affairs in some universities. Certain basic concerns are nevertheless the daily bread of the "typical" dean of faculties. He is, as the formal title implies, an academic or faculty man, and his first or foremost function should be to assist in the development and implementation of curricular plans and programs. Much as the departmental chairman described in Dudley Bailey's essay should be a source of academic dialogue and stimulation, encouraging faculty creativity and leadership to manifest themselves, so, too, should the dean of faculties be a facilitator for other people's ideas. All too often when approached with curricular suggestions he will have to intone the stock phrases about inadequate funds and competing demands, but this should always be his last, not his first, reaction. Many good ideas do not cost additional money, and many others can be implemented with very modest investment of new funds. An effective dean of faculties, no less than an effective chairman or collegiate dean, will always be alert to stimulate and support curricular examination and innovation.

How, specifically, can he do this? First, he can help to move data and information concerning possible academic innovations through the complex channels of communication that can easily become clogged in large universities. Knowledge and ideas, after all, can stimulate action—even in universities! Second, the alert dean of faculties, in cooperation with other deans and program directors, can scout around for the funds and logistical support that a curricular experiment may require. In a well-organized university he is not an academic moneybags. Yet the dean of faculties is appropriately one who, knowing the administrative and personal ins-and-outs of his environment, can assist in the search for needed funds and, equally important, in the matching up of administrators, faculty members, and students who together can accomplish academic objectives. Third, and perhaps most important, the dean of faculties through his expressions of genuine concern and interest in all curricular and faculty questions can contribute to a mood, an atmosphere, that encourages and supports academic innovation. He sits on numerous faculty senate and administrative committees, and he has easy access to university bodies and groups. While he cannot dictate outcomes (no person or agency has this kind of power in the modern, pluralistic university), he can play a large role in setting the agenda and structuring the discussion and consideration of academic issues.

In more formal ways the dean of faculties is likely to have many specific responsibilities. The deans of the undergraduate and professional colleges report to him on faculty personnel matters, chairmanship appointments, and curricular proposals. Moreover, the dean of faculties is commonly charged with direct supervisory responsibilities for a large number of quasi-academic university entities whose primary focus is not teaching but service to the academic programs or to special university and state needs. Thus, at the University of Nebraska his administrative concerns include art galleries, conservation and survey, libraries, and university television. More generally, the dean of faculties works with the president and the university's specialists in budgetary planning and administration in developing the immediate and long-range budgets that are the lifeblood of all academic programs.

Finally, the dean of faculties must be constantly

available to work, usually with the president, toward the solution of what my predecessor aptly described as "crises of the moment." These can encompass virtually any—and every—kind of institutional problem: allegations that a professor has acted unprofessionally; intramural conflicts between academic entities that may impair the over-all university program; or, in this day of social and political tension on the campus, student demands that could disrupt the university's ability to function.

When such crises, which are usually partially subterranean, develop, the dean of faculties will probably be involved as a conciliator and mediator, working with an informal task force to help effect fair and realistic solutions. The problems associated with these sudden crises demand immediate attention, for, if not met successfully, they may endanger the basic well-being of the university. Crises of the moment, it should be added, are often fascinating and exhilarating challenges because of the interplay of incredibly diverse human personalities and political realities; they are also, for all participants, emotionally draining, ruthlessly time consuming, and just plain tiring.

The last sentence implies that the life of academic administrators often involves high adrenalin trips, and the implication is deliberate. But it is also essential to stress that much of the daily life of a dean of faculties and other academic administrators is not at all glamorous or exciting. Quite the contrary; many of the dean of faculties' duties are routine and downright bureaucratic. Frequently, when intelligent and sensitive faculty members come to perceive this, they exhibit an annoyance and impatience because the academic administrator is being insufficiently academic and spending, as they see it, too much of his time on routine housekeeping chores. For example, at the University of Nebraska the routine duties of the dean of faculties include approving payments to faculty for work in special university conferences and institutes that go beyond their normal academic duties, administering accounts for faculty recruitment and institutional memberships, and scrutinizing and endorsing (with the president) every single personnel recommendation form that requires action by the board of regents.

This last duty deserves a few words of explanation. Whenever a member of the faculty or professional staff is appointed, promoted, changed in status, or resigns, legal action by the regents, upon recommendation of the administration, is required. Thousands of such recommendations move through a large university every year, and their proper processing involves many persons and much time. All will agree that this chore, as well as others, must be done by someone. The point, however, is that effective administration, which means administration that not only gets things done as fairly and speedily as humanly possible but also enjoys the confidence of the regents and the public who support the university, *requires* the active involvement of ranking academic administrators in the "nuts and bolts," or the engine room—if you will—of the university.

It bears endless repetition that large public universities are complicated and inescapably bureaucratic organizations.[1] If, as I strongly believe, they are best governed by academic men who choose to become administrators, then those administrators from departmental chairmen through presidents must, commensurate with their responsibilities, be able to manage and administer the day-to-day operations of the university. This means that chairmen, deans, and presidents must become at least part-time clerks able to manage accounts, plan budgets, and superintend personnel matters. They must do this if they are to keep a handle on the complicated activities of a large university and to elicit the cooperation and loyalty of the many thousands of nonacademic personnel without whom universities could not function. An academic administrator, moreover, should strive to

---

1. One of my fundamental assumptions is that there is nothing intrinsically bad or good with bureaus, i.e., bureaucracies; they become necessities when social and organizational needs can no longer be serviced through informal mechanisms. They are either good or bad depending on whether they serve, as fairly and wisely as possible, the needs that justify their existence. The danger, of course, is that bureaucracies may lose sight of the obligations and purposes justifying their creation and come to serve primarily the interests of the bureaucrats. It is, however, perhaps also fair to point out that faculty interests and organizations—and, for that matter, student ones —can also grow into "bad" bureaucracies.

reserve quantums of time for more purely academic matters by delegating portions of his duties, and to do that he must have a working knowledge of the daily, routine operations in his areas of responsibility.

It is, in short, my contention that an academic administrator's partial preoccupation with what we can candidly call bureaucratic procedures and routine is a functional necessity. Administration and policy really are not separable, and the chairman, dean, or president who aspires—as he should—to influencing policy matters must be an effective manager of the daily routine. (By the same token, faculty members and students who wish seriously to influence university policy matters—as they should—must be willing to invest time and effort in helping to administer the day-to-day implementation of their favored policies.)

The dean of faculties, as the preceding passages suggest, is an inevitable bureaucrat. He is not, if he is any good, a bureaucratic cog; but neither is he a one-man academic band. He works with and through (and sometimes around!) the many persons and components of the large university, and thus he is an administrator constantly in relationship with other members of the university. Of these relationships, none are more important or subtle than those he has with the president and the faculty.

It is best to be explicit. To work effectively, the dean of faculties must have his own base of informal, yet real, faculty support, and he must also have wide areas of operating responsibility delegated to him. By necessity, especially because the heavy demands on the president's time severely limit his attention span, the chief executive must delegate *somewhere*. The dean of faculties, who to all intents and purposes is a member of the president's staff, is an obvious candidate. In addition the dean can be influential in shaping presidential responses if the two administrators share, as ideally they should, a common understanding of the university's needs and objectives. In practical, everyday terms this requires that the dean of faculties and the president work together in a close collegial relationship and without particular regard to matters of protocol, status, and ultimate responsibilities. And yet in a university, as in any enterprise that must have internal coherence and has public responsibilities, there can be but one final source of accountability and authority. Whether we examine academic and student affairs or the business, financial, and physical plant side of a university, there must be a chief executive who accepts ultimate responsibility, even for decisions that he has not made personally.

This means, then, that the dean of faculties is unequivocally "an administration man." What else can he be? He is of the administration of the university and must serve it to the best of his ability. After all, properly construed, the administration exists to serve the over-all university, and the dean of faculties in serving the university serves faculty needs and interests. In theory, and fortunately usually in practice, there is an absence of conflict between the dean's work for the president and general university administration and his special concern with academic and faculty affairs. Sometimes, of course, issues and situations may develop where the dean of faculties—or for that matter any academic man—is compelled to confront his personal convictions and internal values. If and when such moments occur, any president, student affairs dean, collegiate dean, departmental chairman, student government leader, or dean of faculties worthy of respect has but one choice—he must be "his own man." The behavior and decisions appropriate to such situations depend on unforeseeable circumstances and intensely personal judgments: here, too, there is no handbook that can prescribe how a dean of faculties should act.

Although a dean of faculties must be an administration man reporting directly to the president, he must also, as his title and responsibilities indicate, be close to the faculty. Clearly, this is an enormously difficult task when there is a faculty numbering more than a thousand that is divided into countless academic specialties and departments (some would call them compartments). The dean of faculties obviously cannot have an intimate and personal relationship with every faculty member but he can, in both general and specific ways, understand their problems and assist in solving them. He should seek as wide personal contacts as possible with individual faculty members, and within the limits of his limited time should be available to help with their problems.

Here again his theme must be that of trying to find ways to say yes, instead of finding excuses to say no—despite the fact that he often will have to say no. He can, in addition, serve as a special communicator between the university administration and major elected faculty committees, such as the Liaison Committee at the University of Nebraska, that are charged with looking after faculty interests.

In all of these relationships the dean of faculties must proceed with discretion and a sure-footed understanding of other relationships. He must be careful not to undermine the positions of departmental chairmen and college deans, who in effect serve as their own deans of faculties. Over the long run the dean of faculties best represents and serves faculty interests by what he is, in his qualifications and past experiences, and by what he does in carrying out his diverse functions. He cannot be a mandated delegate of *the* faculty which, in fact, is no more a monolithic, one-dimensional entity than are *the* students or, for that matter, *the* administration.

Students are yet another concern for the dean of faculties, as they are today for all academic administrators who do not want students to be overly concerned about *them*. His relationships with them, however, are inescapably even more attenuated and indirect than they are with the faculty. With thousands upon thousands of students attending the large university, it is neither possible nor necessary for the dean of faculties to be in regular contact with students. But he will, in common with other administrators and faculty members, see more student faces on the committees he sits on, and he had better have a philosophy for responding to student interests and requests. If he genuinely cares for academic affairs, whose primary thrust after all is education for students, he will long for more contact with students and he will profit from and savor the moments he has to talk with them and listen to their critiques and ideas. He will have infrequent contacts, and he must make a determined effort to keep abreast of both national student trends and on-campus developments. University "crises of the moment" in the seventies will more often than not jointly involve students, faculty members, and administrators, and already it is clear that student initiatives are increasingly influencing academic affairs and stimulating curricular changes. The dean of faculties, therefore, is inevitably and properly involved with students but not, typically, in a direct and permanent relationship.

One reads much these days of the agony of academic administration. According to the news media the position of a dean or a president is a hazardous occupation for which the prime qualifications seem to be a thick hide, a masochistic psyche, and a hot line to the local constabulary. Lists appear regularly in newspapers reporting on the numerous unfilled college and university presidencies with the clear implication that potential deans and presidents are as scarce as volunteer pilots ready to fly covert missions into Biafra.[2] Administrators themselves frequently cultivate the image of being over-worked and cruelly cross-pressured.

We do, indeed, work hard and the pressures get rough, but our laments at cocktail parties are partly ritualistic and partly therapeutic. Complaining is a natural and perversely pleasurable human activity, and

---

2. Typical of this genre of commentary is an article on "the acute shortage of candidates for college presidencies and deanships" by John P. Roche, a newspaper columnist and professor of politics at Brandeis University. According to Roche, approximately 200 college and university presidencies and 2,000 deanships are vacant. He comments, in part:

> . . . a friend who was sounded out by several schools suggests they are having real trouble. He thanked them but politely informed the search committees that he would sooner join the Marines—"there you get medals for valor."
>
> A university president today has an unenviable set of obligations. His primary task is to raise money either from private donors or, in public institutions, from the legislature and ultimately the taxpayers.
>
> The president is also supposed to be an educator, an administrator, a psychiatrist, and—increasingly—a frontier sheriff. As recent sad events indicate, he needs the constitution of an ox and ideally no nerves at all.   ,
>
> Finally, he needs the moral fiber of a Christian martyr because no matter what he does, at least half of his constituents are going to denounce him as a traitor.

See: John P. Roche, "Colleges Hunt for Presidents," *Omaha World-Herald*, 24 August, 1969.

lamenting the burdens of academic administration has particular social acceptance in academic circles. At best there exists a mild faculty (and now student) bias against academic administration, which is often portrayed as a necessary evil and an excrescence on the core purpose of the university—teaching and research. In this atmosphere the prudent administrator may prefer to paint job descriptions that emphasize burdens, impositions on his personal life, and intolerable faculty, student, and public pressures, instead of calling attention to the exciting educational challenges and the fascinating experiences that enliven his work. There is, too, a dose of the martyr complex in all of us: being pitied (and admired) for undertaking unwanted and "impossible" tasks provides its own psychic gratifications.

I submit that the reality is different. Most academic administrators are competent scholars and teachers who have voluntarily chosen positions as chairmen, deans, and presidents. Many—and quite properly so—enjoy the art of academic administration, and they hardly fit the picture of reluctant dragons somehow tricked into accepting burdensome and unwanted responsibilities. And this is the way it should be, for the first qualification of an academic administrator is that he enjoy his work and believe in its significance. To be sure, there are conventional credentials that go with specific positions. A dean of faculties, for instance, should be a man of the academy, perceived by faculty members as a professional scholar. He must have won his academic spurs in the classroom, and in faculty minds he is unqualified for the position unless a respectable number of scholarly publications parade across his professional *vita*. No less important, he must enjoy the personal confidence of the president—his closest partner—and the deans and influential faculty with whom he must work in situations where trust is a priceless commodity.

These qualifications, obviously, are essential but they are not enough. The successful dean of faculties, as the successful chairman, collegiate dean, and president, must have enthusiasm and zest for what he is doing. He must have an instinctive sense, rooted in his prior experience as a teacher and scholar, of student and faculty needs and a keen appreciation of academic politics. Politics is a part of all human organizations, and the dean of faculties must be an academic politician able to work with different people for the sake of over-all university objectives. Above all, he must value the academy not merely for what it is but for what it can be through an endless process of reasoned criticism and self-renewing change.

Academic administration *is* difficult, but so also is creative teaching and pioneering scholarship. It is not, however, an impossible mission bereft of accomplishments and legitimate enjoyments. To argue otherwise is to conclude tacitly that universities are ungovernable and, consequently, doomed to collapse. Despite the many difficult problems that confront the modern American university, no such dismal conclusion is warranted. Contemporary university administration requires principled, academic politicians who are neither afraid of educational visions nor neglectful of social and public realities. Cassandras and Pollyannas are equally unsuited to the task.

◆◇◆ Supplementary Readings ◆◇◆

Mark H. Ingraham and Francis P. King. *The Mirror of Brass.* Madison: University of Wisconsin Press, 1968.

Earl J. McGrath, ed. *Universal Higher Education.* New York: McGraw-Hill Book Company, 1966.

Stephen Strickland, ed. *Sponsored Research in American Universities and Colleges.* Washington, D.C.: American Council on Education, 1967.

Robert L. Williams. *The Administration of Academic Affairs in Higher Education.* Ann Arbor: University of Michigan Press, 1966.

Logan Wilson, ed. *Emerging Patterns in American Higher Education.* Washington, D.C.: American Council on Education, 1965.

THE COLLEGE DEAN

John R. Davis

◆◇◆ CONSIDERING THE MANY FACTORS that exert an influence upon a college—type and size of the institution, institutional goals, geographic location, purposes of the college, budgetary considerations, teaching quality, research efforts, among others—there are probably no two colleges that are alike. Indeed, the strength of education in the United States is due partly to the diversities among institutions and colleges, as well as to their similarities.

The detailed responsibilities and subtleties of a college dean's activities also differ in relation to the above factors; for example, deans at a private institution must devote more attention to alumni and to fund raising than do their counterparts at a public institution. Also, the deans of professional colleges (law, pharmacy, engineering, medicine, and so forth) have a type of professional and social responsibility outside the university that deans of liberal arts colleges do not have. On the other hand, the deans of liberal arts colleges have an internal responsibility that is traditionally different from that of deans of professional colleges. The latter example may be indicative of the reasons that the deans of liberal arts have a lower rank order than deans of professional colleges in the perceived power structure of American universities.[1]

Irrespective of the nature of his institution, a college dean has responsibility to his students, to his university, its president and trustees, to his colleagues, his faculty, and his profession. There are times when he feels additional responsibilities and times when one responsibility must be given priority over another. In general terms, however, the administrator must decide at the outset that he will respond to his direct responsibility in some priority ranking—insofar as his university responsibilities are concerned. These direct responsibilities are to the university through its president and to his faculty. He is naturally and organizationally responsible to the president, and he is also responsible to those who do the work of the college—those who fulfill the purposes of the college. All other responsibilities—including those to students—are somewhat indirect in this context. Thus, one might define organizationally and functionally oriented responsibilities as direct. On the other hand, there are indirect responsibilities that are aesthetic and relate to goal-oriented qualities, such as teaching or environment.

---

1. Edward Gross and Paul V. Grambsch, *University Goals and Academic Power* (Washington, D.C.: American Council on Education, 1968), p. 82.

The Dean's Role

The dean's role, whatever his field, is to formulate and enunciate goals and policies in terms which render their achievement a matter of commitment in the academic community. He is responsible for developing the goals of his college and for contributing to the development of institutional goals. He must pursue the next responsibility of outlining the strategies and developing the opportunities and the resources necessary to achieve these goals.

The paradox of the manner in which these responsibilities are stated may now be apparent. The dean must embrace his indirect responsibilities in order to develop properly his major direct responsibility, namely, the setting of goals for his college or institution. Thus, the dean's indirect responsibilities—the quality of teaching and the curriculum, the needs of society, the economic growth of his region, the aesthetic and ethical values of living—determine the manner and the nature of his collegiate goals, the goals of the institution, the pursuit of these goals, and the functional relation and rank order of influence of the dean within the institution. Those deans who are more sensitive and responsive to their indirect responsibilities will generally be accorded a higher rank order of influence by their colleagues and the faculty and will generally find that their relationships with the president and the faculty will be more harmonious, understanding, and rewarding.

In his speech in 1965 on "A Philosophy of Business

Leadership," Crawford Greenwalt, chairman of the board of E. I. duPont de Nemours and Company, said: "Differences in managerial competence are due not to one person, nor to the few geniuses that cross the stage from time to time, but arise out of the creation of an atmosphere which induces every man or woman connected with the enterprise, no matter what their position, to perform his or her task with a degree of competence and enthusiasm measurably greater than what could be called their normal expectations." Therefore, if the dean can create this atmosphere for his faculty so that they, in turn, may create a similar atmosphere for their students, and if he can stimulate his colleagues to create a similar atmosphere, then the academic community will be in a position to formulate its goals and, furthermore, its success in reaching them is a foregone conclusion. Arthur Kellner, in writing of the Apollo program of NASA, said: "such achievements indicate that most (professional) people are inherently creative and are naturally moved to great heights; it is mainly the restraints placed upon them by their environment that cause performance to be less than satisfactory." [2]

Creating such an atmosphere, which is prerequisite to establishing collegiate goals, requires all those intrinsic attributes of leadership and the existence of, or the potential for, developing the necessary resources. For

---

2. Arthur D. Kellner, "How to Manage Creativity," *Professional Engineer* 39, no. 8 (August 1969): 45–48.

example, the dean must perceive the needs of society and of students, and must be able to state those needs so that his faculty also may perceive and respond to them. There may be disagreements on the priority of the needs or the solutions to problems, but recognition of the need or problem and acceptance of the challenges are the important things. But of even greater importance is the dean's capacity to generate within his faculty the abilities to perceive and to anticipate, so that through his leadership the faculty will have every opportunity to assume those same (or greater) characteristics of leadership enabling it to fulfill its role as a vital force in the institution and in society.

If there is any apparent or real difference between the dean's role as an academic leader and as an administrator, then the dean must choose first to be a leader. If he does not have the perception or the soul to understand the needs of society, of students, of the academic-professional community, of industry, or whatever so that he can lead his faculty to approach these needs, he should not be a dean. Similarly, unless he can lead his faculty to develop collegiate goals and to work toward reaching these goals, he should not be a dean.

In this context, the dean as an administrator should devote his administrative abilities and efforts to the administration of leadership rather than to the administration of routine or recurring details of the college. The latter certainly deserves more than perfunctory attention of the dean; therefore, the administrative details should be delegated to those who can make decisions and who enjoy making things work. To some extent this concept conflicts with J. David Singer's comment on collegial government, except there is agreement with his comment that the faculty should be strengthened and also with many of his concerns about student-faculty-administrative relations.[3] However, there is little enough continuity and strength in administration already without, as Singer suggests, making it hold office at the pleasure of the faculty or of students.

The interpretation of the role of an academic leader depends on the institution. In some cases the dean may feel that he functions best on the national scene; his institution may be willing to contribute his efforts to the national or world good. On the other hand, he may feel that he should remain in close proximity to his students, faculty, or his state. In the first case the institution should be prepared to substitute local leadership for the absentee dean, for neither the faculty nor the students will follow or emulate for long the usually vagrant and uncertain concepts of an absentee dean. In most cases, however, if the dean has generated an *esprit de corps* and a sense of leadership in his chairmen and his faculty, he can devote some of his time and thoughts to national problems so long as he does not alienate faculty.

Even though the dean may be devoted to his faculty and president, and the faculty may be faithful and loyal

---

3. J. David Singer, "Toward Collegial Government in Universities," *Educational Record*, Winter 1969, p. 101.

to the dean, he must delegate some of his responsibilities to others—preferably to other professional administrators rather than to faculty committees. In most instances the functions to be delegated require the decision-making, telephone-calling activities that cannot be performed well by a committee. At the collegiate level, and also at the chairman's level, the professional administrator should be subordinate to the dean or the chairman; for at these levels of the institutional structure, the policy makers and the decision makers are to be served by budget keepers and space planners.

In reality most deans are confronted sooner or later with the decisions of the professional administrator, such as the fiscal analyst in the governor's office, the director of institutional planning, or others. It cannot be stated unconditionally that all professional administrators are subordinate to academic leaders. It is the dean's responsibility to his faculty and his president, however, to generate a rapport with these administrators and to promote an understanding of his collegiate goals. If necessary he should delegate a counterpart in his college in order to enhance this rapport.

In any event, the dean should delegate responsibility for most operational and procedural functions of the college to others—either to subordinate administrators, faculty, secretaries, or technicians. Such delegation is made to protect the time of the dean and the faculty; otherwise, both may become submerged in the operational details of the institution.

Protecting or husbanding the time of the dean, chairmen, and faculty is an operational function that befalls the dean. In spite of the fact that he should not become responsible for too many routine activities, he must be involved just deeply enough to protect his time and to assist in setting operational policy. For example, he must avoid appointing too many faculty committees for trivial matters; he must delegate office detail to his secretary; and, in general, he must preserve his time and the time of the faculty for contemplation, relaxation, and assimilation of new ideas. If financial constraints or other limitations prevail adversely upon his time, the dean in consonance with his institution must determine policy that will remove or reduce the restrictions.

Relationships with the Faculty and Student Body

A new dean is usually selected from among the chairmen or faculty of that college, although there are often valid reasons for searching outside the institution. In any event, the dean is usually the mutual choice of the faculty and the president and, if he comes from the faculty, he has already established strong relationships with his colleagues. These relationships, whether or not the dean is a former colleague, deserve to be strengthened, for it is only through open, thoughtful, friendly, and mutually respected relationships that common goals can be evolved and achieved. A dean may know his faculty; but if the faculty does not know its dean, it has not accepted the dean as its leader.

In some larger universities there are some colleges of over 500 faculty members, which makes a close, personal relationship between the dean and the faculty a rather formidable undertaking. In many colleges a personal relationship between dean and students has already disappeared; this is a regrettable consequence of the population and education explosion. It would be even more regrettable if the dean and his faculty became complete strangers, and every effort, including reorganization, should be made to enhance a productive and warm relationship.

C. E. Weber and his colleagues suggest that authority in institutions of higher learning may be characterized as either bureaucratic or collegial-professional, and they expand this concept by theorizing that the collegial-professional authority results in a stronger, more viable environment for the development of ideas and for project research.[4] On the other hand David C. Knapp, in his article "Management: Intruder in the Academic Dust," deplores amateurs in administration but infers at the same time that academic institutions must adopt the sophisticated methods of modern management so that academic affairs may be conducted effectively.[5]

---

4. C. E. Weber, L. W. Ross, and W. P. McGhee, "Academic Authority and Administration of Research," *Educational Record*, Spring 1966, pp. 218–25.

5. David C. Knapp, "Management: Intruder in the Academic Dust," *Educational Record*, Winter 1969, pp. 55–59.

If the concept of academic freedom is to be preserved, there is no question that management at all levels must be strengthened. In addition personal relationships must be strengthened. But there is no conflict between these two essential institutional qualities. Dressel and his colleagues address their paper to the influence-confidence patterns of academic departments and point out clearly that the success of university operations is due not entirely to logic and statistical data, but also to the personal relationships—faculty feedback, influence, degrees of autonomy, confidence, and understanding.[6] This emphasizes an earlier point that the dean and the faculty must cultivate a close relationship—close enough so that the faculty is not too disturbed if the dean develops an equally close relationship with the president—and an effective system of management which the faculty should expect in any event.

A dean's relationships with students are less critical, because both students and administrators tend to be responsive to social action norms and persist toward common goals. They tend to understand each other and usually can communicate well. Although there are these tendencies, the dean must nevertheless make the effort to maintain this understanding and communication. He may involve himself directly in teaching, advising, giving seminars, or other activities that put him in direct con-

---

6. P. L. Dressel, F. C. Johnson, and P. M. Marcus, "Departmental Operations; The Confidence Game," *Educational Record*, Summer 1969, pp. 274–78.

tact with students. As an example, we at the University of Nebraska have found that meeting with the student board of the college about once each month and having lunch once a week during one semester with ten or twelve students—all with faculty involved—tend to improve communications and relationships markedly.

All deans should have perceptions about student motives and attitudes and should be in a position to anticipate changes and to allocate their efforts and resources accordingly. Most students are helpful and energetic, and a good dean has much in common with good students. However, because most faculty members tend to be responsive to academic professional norms (Weber, et al., *ibid.*), which is unlike student motivation, the dean's responsibilities also include generating a more complete understanding and empathy between faculty and students. This should be a part of the environment of every academic community.

Qualifications for the Dean

Much has been written on the qualifications of a university president but much less on the qualifications of a dean, although the attributes of the two should not differ substantially. As Logan Wilson expressed his view: "Only the Holy Trinity could match the qualifications set forth by most institutions in their searches for academic presidents." [7]

---

7. Logan Wilson, "A Few Kind Words for Academic Administrators," *Educational Record*, Winter 1969, pp. 9–11.

Wilson also points out that there is no substitute for capable and responsible leadership; the main qualification of the dean is simply that he be a capable leader. Leadership is often inherent in the man, but in any event some formal training and sharing the experiences of other deans will make him a still better leader. Ellis L. Phillips details many of the formal programs available to existing or aspiring administrators. In addition to hard work and sacrifice, such programs or other directed and planned efforts should form a part of the continuing education of the manager or administrator.[8] As Knapp put it, "In this environment, the costs of amateurism, both economic and psychic, may be more than we can afford." [9]

Administrators usually enjoy working with people, influencing people, understanding people, and participating in their joys and sorrows; for these are experiences that are fulfilling and rewarding. If a man recognizes and accepts these and truly enjoys this life, he will soon find his place and his responsibility as an academic administrator and will learn along with his faculty about both the pleasant and unpleasant. But they will learn together, and in this way they will build a strong institution and a harmonious college.

---

8. Ellis L. Phillips, Jr., "Toward More Effective Administration in Higher Education," *Educational Record*, Spring 1966, pp. 148–62.

9. Knapp, "Management: Intruder in the Academic Dust," p. 59.

A dean's role in higher education may be an unusual one, for he is least mentioned in the literature of all members of the academic community in spite of his perceived order in the power structure of the institution. Possibly this infers that the role of a dean is usually understood and properly executed and that contributors to the literature accept the dean and do not consider him a major problem. If an aspiring dean really believes this, then his näiveté and peace of mind will charm his faculty and his president for a period of time substantially less than his short tenure as a dean.

◆◇◆ **Supplementary Readings** ◆◇◆

Frank C. Abbott, ed. *Faculty-Administration Relationships*. Washington, D.C.: American Council on Education, 1958.

Charles G. Dobbins and Calvin B. T. Lee, eds. *Whose Goals for American Higher Education?* Washington, D.C.: American Council on Education, 1968.

Archie R. Dykes. *Faculty Participation in Academic Decision Making*. Washington, D.C.: American Council on Education, 1968.

Education at Berkeley. Report of the Select Committee on Education, Academic Senate, University of California, Berkeley, March 1966.

Calvin B. T. Lee, ed. *Improving College Teaching*. Washington, D.C.: American Council on Education, 1967.

Proceedings of the Twentieth National Conference on the Administration of Research. Denver, Colo.: Denver Research Institute, 1966.

Logan Wilon, ed. *Emerging Patterns in American Higher Education*. Washington, D.C.: American Council on Education, 1965.

THE ACADEMIC DEPARTMENT

Dudley Bailey

◆◇◆ IN AMERICAN UNIVERSITIES, the department is where the action is. It forms the center of the teaching, research, and service activities of the university. Departments, within budgetary limitations, decide upon courses and methods of instruction, promote research, and conduct the meaningful intellectual activities with the surrounding community.

In a very real sense, universities are just as strong as their individual departments; in a very real sense, the department is where power lies in the contemporary academic world.

It is temptingly easy to misinterpret this. For naked political power seldom is available to departments, as many an empire builder has learned to his sorrow. Departments, in the final analysis, do not control budgets and have little control over the general planning in universities. In size and budgets, departments grow or dwindle largely despite themselves. Most American universities have departments far larger than their teaching load, research productivity, or community service war-ants; and everyone has departments whose teaching, research, and services far exceed the normal productivity of personnel and budgetary outlay. This harsh fact is probably the most devastating criticism of the administrative system in American higher education, or so many educators contend. But no department can afford to brood over this point; it must learn to think in radically different terms from those which seem to condition academic thought at higher administrative levels.

Departments must think in terms of specific students, of specific research problems, of specific services for the larger community. Overgeneralization is deadly in departmental thinking; insofar as the "wider view" loses the individual student, the individual research problem, the individual service from its focus, that view is not of much service.

It may seem a paradox to say at once that the department is also in grave danger from overspecialization. But it is an obvious fact that many a department has done itself great disservice from overreliance upon its own peculiar "discipline" (a much abused term in academic circles). The English professor who thinks only of belles-lettres, the chemistry professor who thinks only of chemistry, the agronomist who thinks only of agronomy, the educator who thinks only of the "professional component," the marketing professor who thinks only of marketing are of comparatively little value to the intellectual community, despite a popular mythology to the contrary. An agglomeration of mutually unintelligible jargons does not constitute a community of the intellect, simply because it does not constitute a community of any sort.

The paradox is seeming and not real. Overemphasis upon the various "disciplines" is simply another way of avoiding the central problems of the university: the individual students who come to it, the individual research problems shared by community, the individual services the university is prepared to offer the larger community.

Indeed, *sharing* is the key word: departments share in the educating of students, in the attack upon ignorance and fear and prejudice, and in the university's contribution to human life. Whether it is very sensible to organize universities along departmental lines seems to me highly dubious, and my doubts are obviously shared by those who have attempted to break universities out of the departmental cast. But academic molds are not easily broken, and departmental organization no doubt makes for administrative ease. I am quite sure that educational geniuses will come along in good time and find ways of releasing the imaginative and intellectual energies of a university faculty from the bondage of departmental structure; but I do not expect widespread release in my lifetime, unless the restive forces of students, legislators, and citizens combine to force us to do what we should have sense enough to do on our own.

As long as universities are organized as most of them are, the departments must shoulder the burden of the educational enterprise. And this is true, whether depart-

ments like it or not. The rest of the university structure
is at best ancillary, and in many cases irrelevant.

The role of the chairman of a department is ob-
scured in most people's thinking by a widespread mis-
understanding of the nature of a university. At root the
university is not a social organization; it is not a union
of guilds; it is not a joint-stock company; it is not political in its orientation. Nobody really thinks a university
is a sort of country club, and nobody thinks it is a
trade school for skilled craftsmen and technicians. The
administration of many universities has come to resemble
the table of organization of large businesses, but universities are notoriously unprofitable and it takes considerable ingenuity to isolate a set of shareholders apart from
the community at large. I have never heard anybody
suggest that professors or deans or presidents should run
for reelection. The university is not clublike; it is not
guildlike; it is not businesslike; it is apolitical, except in
the profoundest sense. It is a peculiar organization
created by society at large, at considerable expense, to
preserve, refine, and continuously revivify the society's
intellectual traditions; and if it is not intellectually
sound, it is nothing.

Added to the confusion about the nature of the university is the fact that the legal organization of the
university runs counter to the reality of the university's
functions. The notion that intellectual responsibility
really rests with a governing board or a chief administrative officer is patently illusory. To understand the role

of the department or its chairman in a university, it is essential to observe that there obtains a very difficult incongruity of authority and responsibility in the university structure.

I think it is helpful to look on the role of the departmental chairman as analogous to that of a legal advocate. An advocate's first responsibility is to his client; a chairman's is to his department, whose confidence he must fully enjoy. An advocate's task is to discover the best course of action for his client, after weighing the client's resources and the feasible courses of action. He is moreover charged with encouraging new resources and opening doors for new courses of action. Seen in such a light, the chairman's job is not to lead, but to allow for leadership; not to innovate, but to encourage innovation; not to form policy, but to make for a continuous dialogue which will make for intelligent formation of policy; not to control, but to assimilate; not to demand, but to negotiate; not only to talk but also to listen; not to expect too much, but ever to hope for it.

Such a role in a department of any size is a demanding one; it is a full-time job and a noble one. It is also a job nobody can manage on his own; by its nature it demands constant and widespread cooperation with one's colleagues (the concept of a "headship" of an academic department is an absurdity). To do the job, it is especially important that one keep separate the notions of administration and leadership: the departmental chairman can rightly be expected to administer, but leadership in a university, as in any other enterprise, is where you find it; and administration by its very nature does not provide a very likely source of supply.

If one can free himself from foolish worries about leadership, he may discover the qualities that make for a good chairman. And the greatest of these is love: affection for his colleagues and their students, and abiding affection for teaching and learning, in their widest senses. And along with love goes modesty, about his own teaching and research: a chairman should refuse to hire anybody who is not his superior as teacher and researcher, and he should daily express his admiration of his co-workers.

He needs an unfailing sense of humor, one which extends to himself and one without too much cynicism: even in an enterprise dedicated to truth there are abundant human mistakes; even when we are daily chastened for wrongheadedness and arrogance there is more than enough petty pride.

A chairman must be strong in his defense of the freedoms essential to learning and the pursuit of truth, freedoms for both faculty and students; he must be persuasive in the urging of a sense of responsibility which should accompany those freedoms. He must have enduring patience with students, colleagues, and administrative superiors, for changes come slowly in universities. He must be quick to think well of people and judiciously slow to think ill of them. And finally, he must learn never to identify himself with his job: the administrator who takes criticism of his administration as criticism of himself is no longer worthy of anybody's respect or affection.

Seen from this general perspective, the responsibilities and functions of a departmental chairman come to something like the following. First, in respect to his department. The department rightly expects the chairman to mind the paper clips: somebody must assign office space, make schedules, submit budgets and other necessary administrative papers, initiate recommendations for promotion and tenure, and meet the daily problems which arise in the operation of the department. Perhaps more importantly, somebody must organize the considerable work which accompanies the hiring of new staff; somebody must take the responsibility for implementing the means a department discovers for retaining good additions to the staff; somebody must accept as a prime duty the maintenance of those things which lead to high morale in a working department—respect and affection, and intellectual and social security.

A wise chairman soon learns that he can only administer whatever the department as a whole has decided; and the performance of these duties follows from a wide and continuous dialogue with his colleagues. Moreover, he soon learns that authority, like love, is not diminished by delegation—and, as a corollary, that responsibility without authority is both odious and self-defeating. A chairman exists not by the grace of his dean, but by the suffrages of his departmental colleagues. He insists upon a term appointment and a regular review of his position if he has any sense at all. He enjoys his job, but is always ready to leave it.

With respect to his administrative superiors, a chairman must comply with certain obligations. Deadlines have to be met and forms have to be filled; the former are nearly always inconvenient and the latter are rarely entirely sensible. But it is a petty pride that chafes overmuch at these shortcomings. More importantly, the chairman owes his superiors respect, candor, and good temper. Deans have work to do, and in the main they honestly do the best they can; they must insist upon honesty from chairmen if they are to operate well; and they have a right to amiable relationships as well. Duplicity in academic administration leaves a wide and ineradicable mark, and irascibility is rewarded only by weaklings, cowards, and fools. Now, these obligations are reciprocal. In return, the chairman has a right to respect and candor and good temper from his administrative superiors; and he has a right to expect a continuation of the advocate relationship up through the administrative structure: the dean for his college, the president for his deans, the governing board for the university as a whole.

With respect to his colleagues in other departments, a chairman has especial liaison responsibilities. Unless departments work together and keep alive to the possibilities of interaction, universities wither on the vine; and chairmen have the duty to foster the sort of dialogue which creates and maintains the intellectual discourse which is the heart of the university. Deans and presidents talk a lot about this sort of thing; but by and large they are too much removed from the lifeblood of the intellectual community—from the classroom and library and laboratory—to talk about it to any purpose. Even chairmen are less able to talk effectively than their teaching and studying colleagues; hence, they must learn to *foster* meaningful dialogue rather than to *have* it themselves. Unless chairmen, who after all do initiate recommendations for rewards in the academic community, see fit to encourage, by salary and promotion, the interplay between scholars of different departments, the likelihood of a community of intellect and spirit is very dim indeed.

With respect to students, a chairman has obligations of love, respect, and honesty. Students both demand and deserve affection and encouragement; they expect correction but never contumely. They constitute an important part of the university community, not much more transient than faculty or administration and every bit as fully engaged. To ignore their advice about staffing, curriculum, and general policy is irresponsible; to treat them like children is to invite childish reactions; to judge them, we must judge ourselves. Above all else, they must be dealt with honestly. And a chairman faces peculiar difficulties on this score. Problems which arise between students and teachers are in the main problems which a chairman may not hope to solve fairly: he has, after all, engaged an instructor in whom he has confidence, and he is prejudiced, and seriously so, at the outset. If he is wise, he will work for the creation of a less jaundiced avenue of appeal—a committee of teachers and students—in such cases.

Finally, with respect to himself, the chairman has some obligations, too. He owes himself love, and respect, and honesty; and none of these comes ex officio. If his department is happy and productive, he has a right to some self-congratulation; if the chairman's role is not to his liking, he has a right to quit it and turn to doing what he can do well. If he teaches well, he should teach; but good teaching is not bestowed with an academic title, and administrative work in the main is not conducive to excellence in the classroom. He should pursue research if he can do good and meaningful research; to persist in perfunctory research is an act of pride. The pious assertions that a chairman must continue his teaching and research are only pious assertions, and any professor worthy of the title knows that truth is not reached by assertion. Above all else, a chairman must hate falsehood, in all its forms, from the direct lie to the petty pretensions he is especially liable to.

Chairmen are usually appointed by deans, but in the long run what counts most is the judgment of others, and particularly of colleagues and students. Nobody wants to teach or learn in a department which is not improving and maturing in its dedication to the tasks of education.

A good chairman gives his days and nights to the

improvement of his staff and the curriculum, ever mindful of the preciousness of teachers and learners, ever sanguine about the quality of human life and the potential of the human intellect. If he is blessed with good deans and presidents, they will appreciate him. But he had better not worry about that.

Supplementary Readings

Jerome S. Bruner. *The Process of Education.* Cambridge: Harvard University Press, 1960.

John W. Gardner. *No Easy Victories.* New York: Harper & Row, 1968.

Mark H. Ingraham and Francis P. King. *The Mirror of Brass.* Madison: University of Wisconsin Press, 1968.

Paul A. Olson. *A Pride of Lions: America's Cultural Communities and the Preparation of Teachers.* Fourth National Conference, the U.S. Office of Education Tri-University Project in Elementary Education, September 1968. Lincoln: Tri-University Project, 1968.

Joseph J. Schwab. *College Curriculum and Student Protest.* Chicago: University of Chicago Press, 1969.

G. Kerry Smith. *Current Issues in Higher Education, 1964: Undergraduate Education.* The Proceedings of the Nineteenth Annual National Conference on Higher Education, April 1964. Washington, D.C.: National Education Association, 1964.

THE PROFESSOR

Royce H. Knapp

◆◇◆ ABOUT A YEAR BEFORE the outbreak of the student riots at Berkeley, Clark Kerr delivered his widely quoted lectures at Harvard on "The Uses of the University." He presented his conclusions about students and faculties in strong language; his remarks seemed to foreshadow the ensuing years of campus conflict and distress. Kerr said:

> The students find themselves under a blanket of impersonal rules for admissions, for scholarships, for examinations, for degrees . . . . If the faculty looks on itself as a guild, the undergraduate students are coming to look upon themselves more as a "class"; some may even feel like a "lumpen proletariat." Lack of faculty concern for teaching, endless rules and requirements, and impersonality are the inciting causes.

In considering the role of the faculty member in a modern university, it is proper to recognize at the outset that all is not "peaches and cream" in student-faculty relations. Not only is it proper to recognize the irritations, it is well to ask why these relations are, in many instances, strained and discomforting to trustees, financial supporters, faculty, and administrative leaders. Kerr's statement leads one to conclude that faculty and student groups have divergent objectives and goals. In other words, apparently a gulf exists between what students expect to learn and experience and what faculties wish to provide in courses and activities. This theory leaves the administrators somewhere in between as "negotiators," trying to bridge the gap between the trustees, students, and faculty. There is enough information available to show that this is precisely the case. But it is an oversimplification to leave the problem there.

The Changing Professorial Role

It is the thesis of this essay that much of the cause of student discontent does not lie with administrators, trustees, world problems, the federal government, and lack of finances, but rather with the changed role of the faculty in the past thirty years. Explanation of this changing role is necessary if one is to grasp meaning from the current scene, or if one is to make recommendations for change.

Among the factors of change that had a dramatic impact on the university in the 1920s and 1930s was the development of graduate departments in most of the major colleges and universities. In the 1920s the major graduate and professional programs were only getting started, organized, and financed.

By 1940 the "graduate college system" was crystallized. Faculty promotions were based on research; the pattern of graduate assistantships was helping to manage large undergraduate lecture sections, laboratories, and quiz sections; and the system brought prestige and national reputations. In most large universities the objective was to have doctoral candidates welcomed in national meetings, the industrial world, and other centers of learning. No longer did the young Ph.D. think of himself *primarily* as a teacher, or counselor of students. He had to become a producer, a grant-getter, a member of one of the national guilds of scholars.

Chancellor John D. Millet of the Ohio Board of Regents once suggested that the average, bright scholar was influenced more by his national scholarly connections and relationships than he was by members of another academic department or even his college dean. By 1950 a young professor was judged primarily on his publications and the number of doctoral candidates that he had advised. The instruction of undergraduates carried only minimal influence in promotion.

In the 1920s and 1930s another important change took place in the faculty committee work of the university. Whereas the sponsorship of literary societies, service on student advisory boards, and work on student affairs committees once had been considered important, gradually the most important committees became graduate scholarship committees, the research council, the graduate council, and other policy committees of faculty governance. Graduate faculty committees, by 1950, were more important in the career of a young scholar than the interfraternity council or the athletic council. Faculty members who expected to win academic recognition and the major professorships found that they could not spend a great deal of their time on the "mundane work" of student advising, housing, registration, and other housekeeping chores. In most large universities these "chores" were considered menial and they usually were assigned either to the nonresearchers or to young professors.

A new breed of administrator appeared on the scene at this time, a professional who spent all of his time on student development work. The number of counseling officers mushroomed in the post-World War II era, and staff members were added in registration offices to do some of the undergraduate advising. By 1960 the loan office, the housing office, the student finance office, and the student affairs center became the principal contact centers for students.

It would be dangerous to generalize too much, but generally in the larger colleges and universities, students from 1946 onward did not depend upon faculty counseling in many student areas. Grouped into departments, the faculty paid considerable attention to its majors, especially in the junior and senior years when decisions were being made about graduate study. As McGeorge Bundy once observed: "Every department wants its share of the meat."

It is useless to condemn any person or any group for current student unrest. This will produce no solutions. Able, experienced, interested faculty members must again turn their attention to undergraduate teaching and advising. The goal of the faculty member must once again be concern for student development and sensitivity to the amorphous mass of lumpen proletariat. The classroom must become an exciting, adventuresome, and interesting environment since young people seek stimulating and relevant ideas.

At least one role of the faculty member must be to study the student, as well as study with him. The specialists in student affairs have been right—the faculty became alienated from undergraduate work long before the students were alienated from the massive multiversity. It is interesting to note that while the bases for student unrest were being laid, considerable research was being conducted on student life and student problems. Nevitt Sanford led the way in shedding light on the needs, problems, aspirations, and conditions of the students in the modern college and university.

No faculty member has the right to remain ignorant of the current situation. What distresses this professor is that many trustees and administrators have been reading the literature and many faculty members have not.

To be a good college teacher one must work hard at understanding the people he is teaching. This requires more than the administration of a simple questionnaire;

it requires faculty availability outside the classroom; it requires patience, the ability to listen. Many students want to talk about their problems for a long time before they begin to solve them. Others want to toss off ideas and get reactions. Some need confidential advice. Some need specific classroom help. But *every* student has needs.

One does not have to become a paternalist to work effectively with students. Neither does he have to look, talk, and act like a student. One has to do a good job in preparing for class; he must also be available and be reasonable. And a faking of altruism and student interest will be exposed. A faculty member does not have to sacrifice his scholarship or surrender his convictions to win respect from students. Students need committed, conservative, mature men and women around them, as well as some of the younger generation who think with their glands.

The Evolving of a Faculty Member

The old saying that one learns more from what other people do than from what they say tells how most faculty members evolve. After more than twenty-five years of observation, I believe that most young faculty members watch the older, successful faculty members and emulate them not only in scholarship and teaching, but also in manners and politics. An eminent dean once told me that if you could select the top twenty faculty members at a university and at the same time closely observe the new ones, you could tell what kind of an institution you would have in ten years. In some cases this is true; the theory of emulation of the great professor holds. In others, sharp changes come from the newer faculty members who are emulating their advisers and former graduate colleagues. In both instances there is a great value to be gained if those who are models are "first-class people."

Major professors should realize that they are, to a large degree, models and that their behavior may become a life style for the younger faculty member. Mature faculty members who have achieved recognition and success can have a beneficial influence on their younger colleagues, leaving a lasting legacy to their institution. Unfortunately there are senior faculty members who delight in dissecting administrators, trustees, students, the financial situation, travel funds, and even the food in the faculty dining room. Younger faculty members often follow suit.

Senior faculty members can poison the attitudes of their younger colleagues about other departments and colleges in a multiversity. We have heard new young faculty members mouthing the same crummy phrases within a few months that their older colleagues have been using for years. Faculty members are human beings; they are capable of the same distrust, misinformation, and whispering slurs that plague other professional or working groups. But how much better it would be if senior faculty members would take time to point out *some* of the positive contributions of other departments and other colleges, and even—once in a while—put in a good word for an able, hard-working administrator. No college or university is perfect, but we should acknowledge our strengths, our institutional points of pride.

In working with young faculty members, we must help them find some positive, meaningful work in the total institution. Those colleges and universities that wait years before placing younger faculty on major committees are making a serious mistake. Where care has been taken to involve the younger faculty, responsible action and understanding of institutional problems and purposes are the general rule; problem solvers, rather than problem makers, have been developed.

Above all, a faculty member owes his colleagues truth, and the support needed to make them effective. He shares their joys and sorrows; he takes his turn working on the tough committees for the institution's general improvement.

He avoids making promises that he cannot keep; he does not discuss his colleagues in an unprofessional way. He argues with evidence and he retains his sense of values, always respecting the need for human dignity. One must never set out to form cliques and deride other departments and colleges for personal gain. A faculty member should be moral, and he should expect his colleagues to be the same.

He should learn the art of compromise, not as a political maneuver, but as a necessary part of human association leading to institutional progress and development. To be alienated too soon, or when things do not go your way, is to endanger a precious commodity known as departmental and institutional morale. Some faculty members are alienated from their own departmental colleagues early in their careers; they choose to "go it alone." Harboring old grudges is like nurturing the itch; you are always scratching. It is far better to face situations head on and get some resolution.

One should always ask: What can I do to strengthen Professor X? It is easier—and more pleasant—to develop someone than to destroy him. Everyone gains from a cooperating, positive faculty. Everyone loses when there is bickering, suspicion, and selfishness. Besides, we should display our best behavior for our students' sake.

Finally, nothing is more effective than sincere care, concern, and loving kindness in dealing with one's colleagues. All of us must respond to these considerations.

There is no percentage in misrepresenting something to a chairman, dean, or president. Generally, these men and women are trying to make decisions on the basis of evidence, the best evidence available. Faculty members owe it to the institution to help administrators get the best ideas, evidence, and advice available. One need not cavil before administrators, nor seek their favors. One should help them solve problems, the problems of the institution. Open dialogue should be sought by administrators, and the faculty member should effectively participate.

A faculty member must remember that his administrators, and chiefly his president, are dealing with a board of trustees or regents, who are basically public men. These men make demands and they have problems they want resolved. Some trustees can be very demanding, but most of them are broad-gauged people who take a deep interest in their institution's well-being. They do require—and deserve—continuous education and information; this is a major task for the president. I know of one instance where a governing board spent an hour discussing the impact of a juvenile letter written to a newspaper by an irritated—and pompous—faculty member. Whenever a faculty member "vents his spleen" in public, it is bound to require long explanations by administrators to the trustees, for the trustees have the task of explaining the college or university to the general public, and this is no easy job.

In my opinion, caution should be used in presenting personal views on critical issues to the public. There have been few cases, for example, where a professor's beliefs have been accepted by even a majority of his colleagues or students. Most professors are skeptical of change; so are students. Contrary to public opinion, a high percentage of professors are relatively conservative in matters pertaining to politics, sex, and economics. A few may preach new, radical ideas, but they represent a distinct minority.

Nevertheless, public and alumni do judge the college or university by the behavior of its professors. Fortunately faculties have maintained a high standard of behavior over the years. Professors have taken part in civic activities and, in general, they have been exemplary citizens. Public and social groups like to have speakers from the universities; they enjoy them. Faculty members can do much for their institutions when they accept such speaking engagements. They can "sell" themselves as citizens; they can establish the need for research; they can exemplify the kind of teaching that goes on in the institution.

Professors, if properly informed, can explain institutional needs and problems. Sometimes professors can be more effective than the public relations experts and administrators. Many alumni and public men like to talk to professors, believing that it gives them "first-hand" information. Some legislators seek out professors to talk about institutional needs. This, too, can be most effective if the professors retain their professional position and if they do not try to become political. Professors can contribute to institutional public relations.

In a real sense all colleges and universities are servants of the public; they serve the general welfare. The professor, for example, often serves national and international interests by contributing important research in such areas as medicine and agriculture. The world's food supply is being increased by the efforts of agricultural specialists just as health and educational facilities and programs in underdeveloped nations are being improved through the efforts of specialized university professors. In recent years, many colleges and universities have been responding to the urban crisis with trained personnel, comprehensive research studies, and innovative pilot programs. One could devote an entire volume to the listing of such achievements by universities and their people.

The great professors have played major roles, but they must never become common politicians, nor grasping materialists as a few have. Either road leads to loss of esteem by their colleagues, students, and the general public. Increased salaries in the past dozen years have made many professors independent of outside consulting work. There is no reason for a professor to sacrifice his professional and ethical standards for a few extra dollars.

Realizing the importance of his work to the public welfare, a professor's association with his students should take on a new and broader scope; it should become more relevant. At the peak of his career he should be able to work with freshmen, upperclassmen, and graduate students. He should be in a position to contribute to the total institution. One should reach this point by age fifty, leaving many years for the development of other faculty members and students.

A Faculty Member and the Public

For more than twenty-five years institutions of higher learning have found it necessary to inform the general public about their activities and problems. Colleges and universities have long had problems in maintaining harmonious relations with their various "publics" and supporters. In all institutional histories there are chapters that tell of public irritation with the politics of professors or with some aspects of the educational program. In order to avoid such incidents, universities have found it best to provide a continuous flow of information on both institutional progress and problems. An effort is made to enlist the backing of financial supporters—public and private—in maintaining institutional progress.

By the time of World War I, it was necessary for professors to organize the American Association of University Professors. This organizational effort was designed to protect their academic freedom and assure academic due process in maintaining their positions. The fever pitch of patriotism, keyed by the times, often brought tragedy to some professors who maintained a somewhat different position on the war. For example, the harrowing investigations carried on at the University of Nebraska during World War I left deep scars for years. The opinions of professors on politics, sex, economics, or literature can be, and often are, the cause of much carping by the alumni and the public. Somehow these people believe that public utterances of professors are being taught systematically in their classes; they believe that students and others are believing what professors profess as opinions. This simply is *not* so. Students almost always disagree with their professors on major issues.

It is common to hear people in many professions talking about the separation of their life from their work. Rarely does one hear a great professor talk this way. His life is his work and his work is his life. The flow of activity that forms a professor knows very few limits of time or place or space. His research, which opens up new vistas of knowledge and asks and tries to answer profound questions, is part of his total thinking time. Reflecting, querying, testing and retesting, discussing, reading, and listening never leave him bored. The contact with students and colleagues who are also learning and questioning gives him a chance to communicate with other interesting people. Today's multiversity is an exciting, interesting place to be if one will but listen and participate.

To work with youth as they plan and pursue their goals of life is challenging. But even more important it is continuously new and a lot of fun. To know that no two students are ever exactly alike in achievement, aspiration, or endowment is to realize with infinite wonder what magnificent variety exists in mankind. All of this variety enriches and promises a fine future for the nation! And to think that a professor in all the years of his life can be part of it. It is not the duty of professors to mold these lives but to help each life he truly touches to find its own unique values and direction. The professor's job is to query, to listen, to stimulate, not to direct, order, or manage.

Finally, the professor is part of an institution that is playing a great role in human affairs. As he contributes to its life and growth, he develops fundamental loyalties to his colleagues and his institution that last a lifetime. No wonder so many bright young men and women want to be professors!

◆◇◆ **Supplementary Readings** ◆◇◆

Jacques Barzun. *Teacher in America.* Boston: Little, Brown & Co., 1945.

Samuel Baskin, ed. *Higher Education: Some Newer Developments.* New York: McGraw-Hill Book Company, 1965.

Gilbert Highet. *The Art of Teaching.* New York: Alfred A. Knopf, 1950.

Clark Kerr. *The Uses of the University.* Cambridge: Harvard University Press, 1963.

W. John Minter, ed. *The Individual and the System: Personalizing Higher Education.* Boulder, Colorado: Western Interstate Commission for Higher Education, 1967.

Houston Peterson, ed. *Great Teachers.* Brunswick, N.J.: Rutgers University Press, 1946.

Frederick Rudolph. *The American College and University: A History.* New York: Random House, 1962.

THE DEAN OF STUDENTS

G. Robert Ross

◆◇◆ ONE NEEDS ONLY TO PERUSE W. S. Lee's *God Bess Our Queer Old Dean* and scan the headlines in today's periodicals to be aware of the dramatic changes that are occurring in the office of the dean of student affairs. These changes take on additional import when one considers that in the past, traditions, methods, and approaches in higher education have withstood several types of societal changes. No dean can survive without accepting the fact of change.

The role of the student affairs dean in higher education has been an evolving one. Briefly, the changes have followed this pattern. At first the dean was a protector of the status quo, stern disciplinarian, and adviser to men. Additional responsibility came with the creation of a separate office for advising and disciplining women. Specialization and increased demands requiring additional staff further expanded the role to one of director-supervisor. An initial break in the guardian concept of the role came with an awareness of the out-of-class potential for learning. This was followed by the dean acting as creator, initiator, organizer, and administrator of educational and service programs of a complex and diverse nature. Next he became a catalyst for involving others in program and policy formation, and finally the dean has added a new role as innovator for student development.

Not since the American Council on Education committee headed by E. G. Williamson presented the pamphlet "The Student Personnel Point of View" has there been an *accepted* redefinition of educational philosophy for professional staff and faculty working in the administrative areas of student affairs. Edward J. Shoben perceived the crucial need for a philosophical base when he said: "It may be that the basic job of student personnel work, in spite of the not infrequent charges of anti-intellectualism brought against it, is the philosophical one of critically evaluating the role of knowledge in a humane and humanizing education." [1] For many, then, the first inkling that a faculty member turned dean, or social scientist interested in human behavior turned student affairs worker, could actually be considered a teacher having direct input to the core objectives of the institution occurred in the early 1950s. A more recent acknowledgment came from a usual critic of the establishment, the United States National Student Associa-

---

1. Edward J. Shoben, Jr., "Psychology and Student Personnel Work," *Journal of College Student Personnel* 8, no. 4 (1967).

tion, which pointed out, "The Dean of Students is trained in education and counseling, not in jurisprudence." [2]

This change in role may be traced, in part, to the behavior of the dean. No longer does he or may he function as a protector of "Puritan" standards. The basic change from stern disciplinarian to qualified human development officer has occurred. And the change from a one- or two-man office operation to an executive managing scores of professional personnel and thousands of dollars in facilities and operations has occurred. The latter includes movement to student affairs of offices and functions previously administered in the business office and change of emphasis to the achievement of educational objectives.

As institutions have grown, as functions relating to student services have become more specialized, and as specialized expertise has been brought to bear upon educational and human problems, a variety of functions has been assimilated rapidly into the administrative area called student affairs. The term "guidance and counseling" is passing from use, and the passing of the term "student personnel" may not be far behind. The most common way of describing the offices and functions that are included in this administrative area is to specify "those programs and services that affect students outside

2. *College Law Bulletin* 1, no. 7 (May 1969) (New York: U.S. National Student Association):31.

the classroom." There is an exception to this over-generalization: the library in higher education remains a separate administrative unit.

On some college and university campuses, student affairs has institutional responsibility for intercollegiate athletics, the campus police, and security forces. Health centers are included in this administrative framework. The trend toward inclusion of the "student union" continues. Another major shift is the move to student affairs of the central offices of housing, with functional programs including maintenance and food service.

The most common organizational patterns apparently are those grouping such administrative offices as admissions, academic advising, registration and records, housing, union, health center, counseling and other psychological services, placement, scholarships and financial aids (including part-time employment), and student activities (including fraternity and sorority advising, other organizational advising and record keeping, special work with students from abroad, and relations with religious organizations).

Functions which cross the standard office designations are discipline, personal and academic advising, special programs for minority groups, leadership development, research on students, staff training, consideration of individual student irregularities, etc.

The foregoing grouping of functions represents a break with the traditional organizational structure that is being increasingly accepted by universities. There is some indication that larger institutions typically dependent on highly specialized personnel are now considering employing generalists in the central office of student affairs, a pattern which remains typical in the smaller college. For example, the staff person in the dean of students' office who can work with any student who walks into the office, presenting most types of problems, is certainly more desirable than a structure requiring three different offices to deal with three different aspects of a student's problem. In addition, the advising of students individually and in groups opens the door for program planning that may lead to group-individual student development. The focus changes from simply sharing information or outlining rules. The goal is personal development of the individual and further organizational changes may be required. Enlightened deans are experimenting, when the limits of the academy permit, with such designations as center for student development, learning laboratory center, human development center, leadership development office, and volunteer bureau.

The Training of the Dean

One continuing issue for student affairs is how best to utilize the individual staff person with a Ph.D. in counseling psychology. It is debatable whether counseling psychology is the best training for a student affairs dean, but many of our deans do have that background. A long discourse on the preparation of a dean is not in order, but Barry and Wolf; Trueblood; and Ayres, Tripp, and Russell provide information for the reader who wishes a historical review of training in the first instance, an ideal for dean of students' preparation in the second reference, and a statistical summary of deans' training in the United States in the latter instance.

While many of the offices noted earlier need professional people with training in the behavioral sciences, if not in counseling psychology per se, the central student affairs administrative office must have such personnel. Other subgroups in student affairs need preparation and specialization in specific techniques, probably with the master's degree serving as the terminal degree. Yet how to group or organize human behavior expertise remains an unmet challenge.

A current attempt is having the human behaviorist go to student groups wherever they may congregate—residence halls, commons, fraternity houses, coffee houses, ets.—to begin relationships that should maximize individual development. The long-range implication of this movement into other program areas in terms of organizational structure remains unknown, but it is not of immediate concern.

However, the professional in student development, like other humans, seems to function better when responsibilities, relationships with other staff, and guidelines for operation are known, rather than "hoped for" or "guessed at."

Relationship with the President

Understanding, respect, and solidarity describe a good dean-president relationship. The balance that the president maintains throughout his relationships is *acutely* needed in relating to student affairs. The president must be in close contact with students and yet he must not become the dean of student affairs; he must work with the dean on student issues and yet he must avoid creating a demand from students that direct presidential authority be used in all student issues.

Addressing himself to this sensitive relationship, Joseph F. Kauffman said:

> Our foremost concern is the selection and training of the student personal leader—the generalist who will serve as the senior student personnel officer of the institution. He must be sophisticated enough to coordinate testing, health, and counseling services. He must be able to administer substantial budgets and operations, yet be research-oriented and intellectually on a par with senior faculty members. Above all, perhaps, he must be able to represent the president on many delicate and difficult matters. Certainly he must be dedicated to the purposes for which institutions of higher education stand.[3]

While it is viewed as an honor to represent the campus president, restricted effectiveness may result if this aspect of the dean's work becomes disproportional. Wesley P.

---

3. Joseph F. Kauffman, "Student Personnel Administration," *Educational Record* 45, no. 3 (Summer 1964):291–98.

Lloyd emphasized a dean's appropriate preoccupation when he discussed the dean of students in other countries:

> The dean of students is in some countries regarded as the single reflection of the wishes of the university president or board of regents. But, being closer to the students than are other administrators, the dean, if permitted to function properly, could unlock a significant student world to the gaze of professors and to other administrators. As the professor centers his attention on academic subject matter and top administration focuses on financing and controlling a university, the dean of students has only one primary professional concern—the student. It is a major purpose of student personnel administration to assist students in the achievement of maturity and sense of social responsibility. This will not in all cases lead to obedience to university rules nor to conformity.[4]

The former president of the National Association of Student Personnel Administrators, Glen Nygreen, made a similar point when he said, "Student personnel administrators are responsible, independent professionals, oriented toward goals and the maintenance of standards and values."[5] Nygreen further pointed out that this identification of the dean is in direct conflict with those

---

4. Wesley P. Lloyd, "The Dean of Students and the University in the International Setting," *NASPA Journal* 6, no. 3 (1969):139–44.

5. Glen T. Nygreen, "Professional Status for Student Personnel Administration?" *NASPA Journal* 5, no. 3 (1968): 283–91.

critics who contend that "student personnel administrators are employees of the institution and as such represent the administrative establishment."

Relationship with the Student Body and the Faculty

A trend to move the dean of students out of a disciplinary role, or at least to minimize that role, has begun. Caleb Foote and Henry Mayer, discussing the aftermath of the Berkeley revolt, referred to the University of California Study Commission on University Governance which mentioned the conflicts of interest that were built into the role of the dean of students at the University of California:

> Under conditions at that time, the Dean of Students might be a student's confidential adviser or become his prosecutor, or be an investigating magistrate, or serve as a trial judge using procedures of his own devising, or impose sanctions which may or may not be reviewable by anyone else.[6]

In view of these conflicts, the study commission recommended that the dean of students no longer play a major role in discipline. The commission contended that the judicial function of the office should be transferred to a student conduct court, and the disciplinary role should be transferred to an agency that would act as the proescutor in student disciplinary cases.

---

6. Caleb Foote and Henry Mayer, *The Culture of the University: Governance and Education* (San Francisco: Henry Mayer & Associates, Jossey-Bass, Inc., 1968).

The commission saw the most important function of the dean as "that of helping a student make the most of his educational experience." Describing his role, the commission stated:

> He is in the best position to assist the student to overcome personal, financial, or bureaucratic obstacles to the best utilization of the student's educational opportunities, and he is in a key position to guide students to specialized counseling facilities when such referrals are appropriate.

When the generation gap is carefully analyzed, it seems to focus on the staff and faculty in higher education who come in daily or frequent contact with the college student. This relationship is where the fears and concerns of parents, the general public, and the governing board are brought to bear on the staff, which is faced also with the corresponding needs, desires, hopes, and anxieties of the young person in our society. The dean of student affairs and his staff are at the vortex of these anxieties, concerns, changes, and fears. Never before have professional staff and the student affairs dean been challenged to such a degree to maintain communication and to contribute to the accomplishment of institutional objectives with primary attention on development of the individual.

Hopefully, the student affairs staff, including the dean, has been able to make the necessary adjustments to work with a variety of students, with a variety of value systems, and with a variety of life styles. The dean has never before had to work with such a variety of students in higher education. And the diversity will continue to grow as colleges and universities reach out to groups of prospective students heretofore not included in large numbers in higher learning.

The successful dean of students seems to be moving away from the traditional patterns of office operation. He no longer waits for or expects students to come to him. He seeks ways to meet with students personally. For example, the dean might hold publicized coffee hours each week in a student setting, at which any student could join in and raise any question. Another approach currently in use is the selection by the dean of any ten or twelve students to participate in a breakfast for an open discussion with no agenda. By using such methods the dean regularly and systematically would *involve* students in the issues of the academic community. It will be an unhappy faculty member or dean who does not accept a rapid increase in equitable student participation in the policy formulations of the academy. A recent discourse on the topic is included in the chairman's report from "The President's Commission on Student Involvement in Decision-Making" at Cornell University.

The importance of the dean's having skills in group dynamics is growing even though this skill should have been in his "bag of tools" for the past three decades. The increased impetus seems to result both from the high demand on the dean to be in contact with more students and the current interest of students in human relationships.

At a recent meeting of vice presidents for student affairs, the importance of communication with the faculty and general student body was discussed in detail. One of the dean's continuing problems is to gain an understanding of the 96 percent of the student body with whom he has little or no contact. Typically the dean has frequent contact with student leaders and severe problem cases. To understand the larger group requires systematic efforts by the chief student affairs officer, as well as clearly defined channels of communication with staff. No dean can resist the demands on his time for interpreting and commenting on campus disruption, its causes, proper reactions to it, and the cures for it. Meeting with parents, alumni, friends, and the general public for discussions of the "youth revolt" is a top priority today. As Kauffman said:

> The Dean of Students today has new roles both inside and outside the university. On the *outside*, he is sought after by the mass media, as well as by puzzled alumni and others, to *interpret* the new student phenomena—be it drugs, protest, hippies, or the new morality. If he is not careful, the dean may find himself catering to the often-perverse fantasies of those who delight in imagining the worst. We need the skill and insight to interpret student needs and to be their advocate and not merely apologist.[7]

7. Joseph F. Kauffman, "The Next Decade," *NASPA Journal* 6, no. 1 (1968):21–23.

Kauffman believes that the dean must challenge those processes, assumptions, and traditions which no longer serve the needs and best interests of today's or tomorrow's students. The need is paramount to evaluate constantly and to encourage departments and sympathetic academicians in the behavioral sciences to assist through research, exploration, and communication in making the universities better places for student development.

Articles and books have been written about the relationship of the faculty and student affairs staff. Generally the student affairs staff is preoccupied with the problems of this relationship, believing they lack status and understanding. Staff members sometimes believe that the value they place on the individual student is being questioned by members of the faculty. Some basis of cooperative endeavor between academic and student affairs deans, between faculty and student affairs staff, is essential. Once again, student affairs personnel must reach out—they must go to the faculty. A little known phenomenon is that many of the financial and other rewards teaching faculty may have received for special, effective, and time-consuming service to students were initiated by student affairs personnel.

Issues Facing the Dean

Some of the major issues that are confronting deans of student affairs around the country, summarized briefly, are:

1. Special needs regarding programs for minority groups. Questions about favored attention for minorities will be asked of higher education for several years ahead. In many instances these concerns will be brought into focus by minority students. The diversity of backgrounds found among these students most certainly adds to the complexity of the problem.

2. Lack of understanding—both internal and external —of the *potential* for effective learning that exists via the student affairs approach or student affairs programs.

3. Student efforts to gain complete control of out-of-class programs and dictate the policy formation for student life. Partly as a result of the lack of understanding of the potential and partly as a result of the indifference that exists on many campuses, more and more educational programming may be abandoned by the faculty and staff, leaving "voids" to the aggressive minority of students. In some instances, students may do a better job in development programming, but generally the training and experience of the student development scholar is invaluable.

4. The student attack on *in loco parentis*. By "kicking a dead horse," this attack may result in increased legalism on the campus. For many institutions, the question of acting in place of parents was resolved *negatively* several years ago. It is essential to note that the basis for the concern of faculty and staff with the out-of-class behavior of students is *educational*. This distinction lies at the heart of many conflicts on campus today. For a

thoughtful presentation from the courts, which recognizes the difference in educational goals and processes and the societal system of maintaining order, attention is called to the "United States District Court for the Western District of Missouri En Banc."

In this student-faculty and staff conflict, many are not aware of the distinction between *authority* and *power* as distinguished in a recent issue of the Association of Governing Boards journal by Robert A. Nisbet. His article "When Authority Falters, Raw Power Moves In" is enlightening. Members of the academic community need to be reminded that if they do not act on pressing problems, the society at large will, resulting in further inroads on institutional autonomy. It is interesting to observe human organization struggling to remove a particular external control, only to find that after success, another control group moves into the newly created void. For example, certain institutions, at the request or demand of some students, eliminated regulations on off-campus housing only to have the city move in with a similar ordinance. Thus, the policy making simply moved from within the academic community to an external societal body.

5. Development of a new policy for student financial assistance. With millions of dollars being loaned to students and with the loans carrying repayment periods up to twelve years, there is great need for a philosophically and economically sound policy.

6. Selection of staff members. This remains one of

the most, if not *the* most important function of the dean. As stated earlier in the essay, staff members in student affairs are in the "eye of the storm"; thus, their training, experience, stability, and maturity are crucial to the success of student-related programs. A slightly recognized, but important, staff characteristic that is sought by the dean is basic skill and interest for financial management.

Today's student affairs leader must bring together, in the context of higher education, knowledge of the behavioral sciences. He must focus attention on the student and utilize the philosophical framework of the wholeness of the student and the individual differences of the student. He must take the student as he is, utilizing the skills of group work, administration, and research. The student affairs leader must serve as the center for understanding the student and as a resource person for faculty, students, and other administrators.

◆◇◆ Supplementary Readings ◆◇◆

A. R. Ayres, P. A. Tripp, J. H. Russell. *Student Services Administration in Higher Education.* Washington, D.C.: U.S. Government Printing Office, 1966.

R. Barry and B. Wolf. *Modern Issues in Guidance-Personnel Work.* New York: Bureau of Publications, Teachers College, Columbia University, 1957.

"In the United States District Court for the Western District of Missouri En Banc." General Order on Judicial Standards of Procedure and Substance in Review of Student Discipline in Tax-Supported Institutions of Higher Education.

Gordon Klopf, ed. *College Student Personnel Work in the Years Ahead.* Washington, D.C.: The American College Personnel Association, 1966.

W. S. Lee. *God Bless Our Queer Old Dean.* New York: G. P. Putnam's Sons, 1959.

Robert S. Morison. *The Chairman's Report: The President's Commission on Student Involvement in Decision Making.* Ithaca, N.Y.: Cornell University, 11 June, 1969.

Robert A. Nisbet. "When Authority Falters, Raw Power Moves In." *AGB Reports* 12, no. 10 (July-August 1969).

E. G. Williamson, et al. *The Student Personnel Point of View.* American Council on Education Studies, Series VI, vol. 13, no. 13. Washington, D.C.: American Council on Education, 1949.

STATE GOVERNMENT IN
HIGHER EDUCATION

Gene A. Budig

◆◇◆ WHILE SERVING AS CHAIRMAN of the National Governors' Conference, North Dakota Governor William L. Guy observed that "the balance of power in state government is a prized possession." He said that "true power" is held by the branch of government which exerts "the most influence over the budget process—this is where destinies are shaped." [1] It is significant, then, to note that respected students of state government generally believe that gubernatorial influence on state budgeting has never been greater than it is today. They believe that the governors represent the dominant voice in state government.

State Senator Richard Marvel of Nebraska said that "in many ways the legislative branch of state government has abrogated its responsibilities by refusing to properly staff its operations, especially in the area of budgeting." [2] At a time when state legislatures have

1. Proceedings of the 1967 National Governors' Conference, published by the Governors' Conference.

2. Interview with State Senator Richard Marvel of Nebraska, 29 May, 1969.

been reluctant to act, governors have taken bold and impressive strides to upgrade their executive staffs. The nation's governors have gone out and recruited a cadre of young, talented professionals, individuals who plan to remain in state government and plan to remain in the administrative branch of it. In states such as California, Michigan, and New York the executive branch has attracted promising administrators from major corporations. Salary schedules were amended—and dramatically—to make state government competitive for these people.

Brevard Crifield, executive director of the Council of State Governments, said there can be no doubt that the administrative branch of state government has taken the leadership in the past five years, and he believes that these strides have done much to upgrade state services and the responsiveness of state government. He also contends that this progressive approach is serving to spur legislators into a more aggressive position. But it is unlikely that the administrative branch will lose its dominant standing for at least the next five to seven years.[3]

As the *New York Times* said: "It takes years, not months, to build a good staff at any level of government. This is especially true in state government." The *Times*, in the same editorial, credited the governors for having "considerably more insight" than their legislative col-

---

3. Interview with Brevard Crifield, executive director of the Council of State Governments, 4 June, 1969.

leagues in filling staff positions. According to the newspaper, legislators historically have been too concerned with false economy and petty policial issues. "Governors realize that it takes money and people to make state government work; legislators—or at least too many of them—do not realize this," the *Times* claimed.[4]

Interestingly enough, a recent survey of governors shows that they favor the upgrading of staff for legislators; they expressed the belief that universal strength in state government is good for all of the government branches; and a number of the governors said that the legislators have been "much too stingy" with themselves.[5]

Public college and university presidents are very much aware of the new and imposing position of influence that the governors now occupy. In a study involving twenty-one of these collegiate administrators, it was acknowledged that strong gubernatorial support is necessary if the presidents are to move their educational programs forward.[6] Without the governors' active backing, the administrators contend that they would be politically stymied, seriously handicapped in their efforts to secure legislative support for adequate appropriations. They all agreed that gubernatorial influence has reached

---

4. *New York Times,* 9 April, 1968, p. 22.

5. Forty-two of the nation's governors participated in this survey which was conducted by the author in December 1968.

6. Twenty-one college and university presidents participated in this survey which was conducted by the Chancellor's Office of the University of Nebraska in January 1969.

a new high in state educational matters, and they generally believe that this influence has been used for the betterment of public higher education.

These administrators have had an unprecedented amount of dialogue with the governors in the past five years, and they have found them to be "unusually sensitive" to the needs of public colleges and universities. They are optimistic about future relationships with the executive branch of state government.

The collegiate administrators also reported that:

1. The governors are troubled—deeply troubled—with the current crisis being experienced in the urban areas; they are aggressively looking for solutions, ways to "keep the lid on" an explosive social and political situation; they are looking to the institutions of higher education for leadership.

2. Programs in urban affairs have caught the attention of the governors; such programs, or ones that will come to grips with the problems of the city and its people, are likely to be supported by governors and funded by state legislatures.

3. Expansion of vocational education and the creation of new community colleges are under serious study by the governors who generally regard such areas as likely to yield positive returns.

4. The governors are anxious to receive recommendations for educational programming that seemingly hold promise for tangible action; their mood is generally receptive and apparently conducive to action.

5. The governors are determined to explore new routes of social research, to find ways in which man can learn to

live better with his neighbor. Schools of social work appear to enjoy favor with the chief executives.

6. The governors are in no mood to abrogate their responsibility to the federal government, although a number of them have expressed a desire to work "much closer" with the various federal agencies.

7. A number of the state leaders believe that outstanding urban colleges and universities will have to be developed in virtually all of the states; these campuses, governors contend, would be asked to attack urban problems with the same zeal that their academic predecessors applied to the problems of rural America fifty and seventy-five years ago.

8. Not many of the governors claim to be experts in suggesting what should be done or attempted on the campus. They have suggested that those educational administrators who had hopes of continued gubernatorial support for their institutional budgets should find practical solutions and make appropriate recommendations.

9. Most of the governors seemed inclined to support research that was designed to enhance industrial development, which they believe means jobs—jobs for the disadvantaged, the poor and the Negro.

These observations have been substantiated by several recent studies of gubernatorial views on major issues in higher education. One of the studies clearly shows the governors to acknowledge that research activities on the campus have been instrumental in moving the state and national causes forward.[7] But they do believe that the time is right for a massive reassessment of the priorities

7. Forty-four of the nation's governors participated in this survey which was conducted by the author in February 1969.

being assigned to the research on the campus. They continue to express a strong willingness to support higher education, despite its heavy and growing economic demands. Quite frankly, the governors feel that it holds the key for a united society. But they are calling for more and quicker results from their capital investments. They, in some instances, believe that it is a matter of survival for the nation.

Those governors surveyed said that they would rather defend budgets for higher education than requests from other state agencies such as welfare and roads. They report little public resistance to increased educational budgets. And as New Jersey Governor Richard J. Hughes said: "If the nation's colleges and universities can solve our impending social crisis, they will have the unyielding support of the public for many generations to come." [8]

Public college and university administrators have become concerned about their institutional prerogatives in recent years; they fear possible invasion by state government. It is important, then, to cite another survey which involved forty-five of the nation's governors. The study clearly indicates that the governors believe college and university campuses in their states should be permitted to develop their own character within the framework of virtually unrestricted autonomy.[9]

8. Ibid.

9. Forty-five of the nation's governors participated in this survey which was conducted by the author in September 1968.

The chief executives express a firm resistance to any temptation to throw campus policies and activities into the political arena, despite mounting public concern over the life on the campus. While governors should participate in charting the course of higher education in their states, they believe, they should not interfere with administration or conduct on the campus. That should be left to the governing bodies of the institutions themselves.

The study clearly indicates that state chief executives follow collegiate developments with much the same vigilance that college presidents might use in studying the patterns of student unrest. For public opinion is, to a great degree, a governor's business. Failing to sense it, guide it, and gain its support, the governor's program —even his political life—is in jeopardy. Although campus developments most certainly could affect a governor's political career, almost all of those polled seem likely to continue a "hands off" policy with respect to possible gubernatorial intervention.

Former Michigan Governor George Romney, now secretary of housing and urban development, put it this way: "The State of Michigan has a strong tradition of institutional autonomy which generally insulates governors from campus politics. I think this tradition is healthy." Governor Norbert Tiemann of Nebraska believes a governor should not "become directly involved in campus political activity." Nor, said he, "should the governor set executive policy for a state institution, except as he may do so through a coordinated program for higher education in the state or through indirect budgeting control." Missouri Governor Warren Hearnes said it would be inappropriate for "anyone other than duly constituted boards and commissions to be directly involved in the details of individual campus policies and activities."

However, Governor Paul Laxalt of Nevada expressed his belief that governors should exert leadership if campus policies and activities "run counter to serving national-state interest." In the final analysis, Governor John Dempsey of Connecticut said, "campus activities and policies are better left to the governing boards of the respective institutions. Concern with allocations for higher education seems a much more productive area of attention of the chief executive."

There are other reasons for this gubernatorial neutrality. The nation's governors are politicians; they have to be elected and this takes time, lots of time. As the late Alfred E. Smith of New York once said, "A good governor . . . or one who stays in public office . . . spends the lion's share of his time mending fences." [10] These public officials freely admit that they do not have the time to intelligently inject themselves into campus affairs. They do not have the time to become proficient in the intricate study of faculty and student behavior. Quite frankly the students, in many ways, perplex them, leave them with a sense of uneasiness. The collegians of

---

10. *Washington Post*, 9 March, 1922, p. 2.

today are proving to be too unpredictable, and it is no secret that politicans prefer to deal in the realm of hard, definable realities.[11]

The governors most generally prefer to "go along with" the professionals on the campuses, the deans of student affairs and their staffs. There are distinct advantages in doing so. The odds for success are greater when student problems or disturbances are handled by the appropriate campus officials. And the delegation of authority by the governor to the campus gives him an acceptable and professional "out" should a situation backfire. In such instances, campus autonomy becomes a political asset to the governor.

Most governors admit that they do, and agree that they should, make indirect educational policy decisions through the budgeting process.[12] "Funding of programs is the most obvious policy instrument available to a chief executive, and his concern in this area must be permanent," former Governor Tim Babcock of Montana pointed out. Governor Guy said that the governors "can exert great influence in providing leadership in financing higher education from state funds." Governor Hughes of New Jersey believes his colleagues must "provide the continued political support to public universities and colleges in their quest for excellence." Such support, he says, "must, of course, be largely in the area of secur-

---

11. Joseph F. Kauffman, *The Student in Higher Education* (New Haven, Conn.: The Hazen Foundation, 1968), pp. 3–15.

12. Governors' survey, September 1968; see above n. 9.

ing adequate finances, but must also be in the direction of seeking a public consensus on the importance of higher education in the state. Unless violation of the law has occurred or is threatened, governors should never interfere with activities on campus."

The chief executives of state government agree that they should limit their direct control over higher education to the financing field. "I do not believe that he (the governor) should go very far beyond budgetary control in his direct relationships with an institution of higher education," Governor Tiemann of Nebraska noted. "This is a governor's primary responsibility," Mr. Romney agreed. "The governors should limit themselves to the funding or finance aspect of higher education and to general educational policies of the state in the area of higher education," United States Senator Harold Hughes insisted while serving as governor of Iowa.

According to the governors, astronomical needs of higher education will continue to tax state revenue and ingenuity. In fact, nearly two thirds of the governors surveyed believe that the federal government will need to increase its financial assistance if the states are to meet their educational commitments during the next decade. These governors contend that the federal government can hardly afford not to increase its allowance to the states in view of the current national goals and objectives.[13] Governor John A. Love said, for example,

---

13. Proceedings of the 1968 National Governors' Conference, published by the Governors' Conference, pp. 47–74.

that it is doubtful whether his state of Colorado will be able to continue to expand its educational opportunities, particularly through new community colleges, and to upgrade universities to the desired level of competence and adequacy without "substantial federal assistance."

It is interesting to note that under the first state constitutions, supreme power rested with state legislatures. The powers of state governors, by contrast, were sharply circumscribed. It was common for the legislature to appoint the governor for a short term of, perhaps, one year. During this early period, governors were quite weak and they were under close check by the legislatures. Today the positions of the legislature and the governor are virtually reversed.

According to Professor William J. Keefe, a number of circumstances and powers are linked to the emergence and development of the governor as "a legislative leader." He claims that the governor's pre-eminence in state politics came "more from an accretion of influence than from wresting leadership from the legislature." [14]

The major constitutional power of the governor is the veto which is authorized in every state except North Carolina. Most of the governors also have an item veto on appropriation bills. Efforts to override a gubernatorial veto are rarely successful.

"A distinctive source of the governor's ability to lead

---

14. Alexander Heard, *State Legislatures in American Politics* (Englewood Cliffs, N.J.: Prentice-Hall, Inc., 1966), pp. 52–65.

the legislature is in his authority over budget making," Professor Keefe asserted. In practice, however, legislative review of the executive budget is an uncertain element of the budget process. Many students of state government believe that too often legislative review of the executive budget is "cursory, haphazard and uninformed." It is common for the governor to lose on some of his budgetary recommendations, but he generally wins victories of wide-ranging significance. His recommendations, in most instances, serve as legislative guidelines.

It is fair to say that crisis dramatizes the governor's responsibilities. He alone can focus sharp attention on state issues. On the other hand, it is rarely possible for the legislature to speak with a single, united voice. But California Governor Ronald Reagan cautions that "it is the legislative branch of government which appropriates the dollars; it would be a serious mistake to underrate its importance in the governmental process."

◆◇◆   **Supplementary Readings**   ◆◇◆

Richard M. Abrams. *Conservatism in a Progressive Era*. Cambridge: Harvard University Press, 1964.

Gene A. Budig. *Governors and Higher Education*. Lincoln: University of Nebraska Publication, 1969.

Jack M. Campbell. "Is Higher Education in Trouble with the Public?" *AGB Reports* 10, no. 8 (May 1968).

Edward Gross. *University Goals and Academic Power*. Washington, D.C.: American Council on Education, 1968.

Allan Nevins. *The State Universities and Democracy*. Urbana: University of Illinois Press, 1962.

Coleman B. Ransone, Jr. "Political Leadership in the Governor's Office." *Journal of Politics* 26 (1964): 197–220.

PUBLIC RELATIONS

George S. Round

◆◇◆ GOOD PUBLIC RELATIONS is essential to any public college or university if the intellectual community is to operate effectively and achieve its objectives of free inquiry and investigation. There must be understanding of what higher education is all about; there must be acceptance of its unique position in today's society.

Every institution of higher learning has public relations woven into its fabric. Its public relations may be unorganized or organized; it may be ineffective or it may be highly effective. Before there can be effective public relations, there must be a clear understanding of the place of the college or university in the society it serves. Understanding must come before acceptance and precede a willingness to properly support higher education financially. Good public relations is a tool to help achieve the hopes, dreams, and aspirations of the academic community. This does not mean that the principles of higher education need be compromised in any way.

The Facets of Public Relations

What does the term public relations mean? There are at least fifty definitions. It conjures many different images. One of the pioneers in the profession calls it the "engineering of consent." Others call it "image making"; still others say it is the sum total of impressions the public has of any given institution.

Whatever the definition, no institution of public higher learning can say as industry once did: "The public be damned." It is the public that provides the resources for the institution to operate. Public relations, in my opinion, is:

The student's impression of his professor.

It is the gratitude of a mother whose child has been saved at a university-operated nursery for premature babies.

It is the pleasure—or displeasure—of a department store clerk upon reading a statement issued by someone associated with the university.

It is the response of a filling-station operator to a conversation with a university professor.

It is the wonderment of a bookkeeper witnessing, for the first time, the night sky as seen from a comfortable seat in a planetarium located on a university campus.

It is a whole host of intellectual or emotional responses of citizens, from all walks of life, to the university and the people who work there.

A public relations program, on the other hand, is a systematic effort to stimulate an interchange of information and ideas between the university and the society that nurtures it. Since we are living in a society in which individuals are reasonably free to choose between belief and disbelief, between understanding and nonunderstanding, between acceptance and nonacceptance, we cannot force our citizens to believe that which they do not wish to believe. Therefore, it is the everlasting task of a university to persuade citizens to continue to think of higher education as a force for good, to continue to believe that the university is, in one way or another, contributing to the enrichment of their lives. All of this must be accomplished without cheapening or distorting the basic values of the institution.

The public relations task is an awesome one because we must address the citizen at his level of interest. This involves sustaining and—most certainly—deepening the image of the university to the small town banker, whose sole concern may be the football team. Or to the farmer, whose interest may be confined to the help that he receives from the county agent. Or to the father whose worries may center around his son's ability to earn a degree. And then, of course, there are many who have no apparent interest in the university. Why should we be concerned about these people? We should be concerned for at least two reasons.

First, the direction of public institutions of higher learning and their economic health are determined by the breadth of understanding that people have of higher education. Second, we cannot expect informed support from a citizenry that is not encouraged to inform itself about the university. We have not reached, or even come close to reaching, that happy state when significant numbers of our citizens come forward to inform themselves independently.

If we accept the notion that our public relations is the sum of all the impressions derived from all our interests and activities, still another question remains to be answered. In creating these impressions, should we sing in one great swelling chorus, each of us voicing the same note?

The answer is no, an emphatic no. Any college or university is characterized by freedom to inquire—and to speak—in its teaching, research, and public service programs. Freedom will inevitably yield honest differences of opinion and earnest debate of ideas. Yet the public must understand these principles if it is to accept the university and support it financially.

A good public relations program should have four general objectives:

1. Stimulating an interest in the university
2. Developing an understanding between the people associated with the university and the people the university seeks to serve
3. Providing a clear understanding of what the university is and what it seeks to accomplish
4. Encouraging an appreciation of the university's accomplishments and fostering an acceptance of the necessity for continued support

In substance, we believe that these objectives are best served by a free flow of information; we believe in utilizing every device to stimulate discussion of all subjects that bear upon the general welfare of the university.

Under no circumstances should public relations be viewed as a censoring agency for the faculty, students, and staff. One must realize that a university will always be a source of both favorable and unfavorable news; this is a condition of freedom of communication that must be accepted. Suppression of information is not a part of any good public relations program.

The Public Relations Department

Today public relations is an integral part of any college or university administration, although the organizational facet may differ from school to school. Emphasis on good public relations has rapidly increased in the past twenty-five years, much as it has in industry, commerce, and government. Our chief professional society is the American College Public Relations Association. It began as the American College Publicity Association. Practitioners at that time were primarily press agents and they were involved in operating press bureaus. More recently, the field has broadened with increasing emphasis on areas such as development and fund raising.

Within most universities, the central agency responsible for public relations may be known as the Public Relations Department, the Office of Information, the

Office of Public Information, and the Department for
Development and Fund Raising. There are other titles,
too.

The organizational pattern for public relations will
vary with relation to the emphasis given to the program
by the chief executive officer of the institution. Today,
the chief officer has to be concerned with public relations if his institution is to survive and move forward.
Gone are the days when the chief executive can delegate
publicity chores to a special office and thereby dismiss
his concern in the area. After all, the chief executive
officer is the real public relations director. He must
devote considerably more time to this area than he did
in the past. Efforts in public relations must be incorpo-
rated into the day-to-day operations of the institution.

Furthermore, the head of a college or university
should realize that a public relations program, however
organized, must be built on a sound program of education. No public relations program will succeed unless
it effectively communicates a sound educational program.

In order to realize success, a public relations department must have access to the details of administration
and enjoy the total confidence of the administration.
That confidence, however, must be earned; it is not something that comes automatically.

The Program and Its Publics

In all public relations programs, there are many
different "publics" to be served. They include the

faculty and staff, students, mass media, community leaders, parents, alumni, legislators, state government, federal government, and the professions. Communications are achieved through the printed word, radio and TV programs, through house organs, personal contact, public service programs, speakers bureaus, and through a host of other devices.

Faculty members, whether they acknowledge it or not, are automatically involved in public relations within their institutions. Without compromising their academic principles, they can make a positive contribution. By taking a personal interest in their students, as all good teachers do, they can improve their institutions' relations with the public. By refusing to take such an interest, and being interested only in research and publication, they can generate negative reaction from both their students and the general public. The university has an obligation to keep the lines of communication open between faculty and administration. Some institutions maintain such communication through a variety of methods, including a regularly published house organ.

Faculty members can contribute to good over-all public relations by serving on advisory committees on public relations. They can—and many do—seek the advice and counsel of public relations professionals on matters of public concern. However, no public relations office should be involved in strictly academic affairs.

The student population is a critically important public. Students can help to create favorable or unfavorable relations with the public. Involving students in public relations is desirable. Recent student unrest, whether justified or not, created many problems for institutions of higher learning. This was particularly true where violence and the destruction of property occurred.

A survey by the National Association of State Universities and Land-Grant Colleges in July 1969 reflected state legislative responses to campus disorders. A number of state legislative bodies reacted by lowering financial support and by enacting repressive or restrictive legislation. Antiriot bills were introduced in many states. Investigations were launched. Photographs appearing in the national press showing students leaving a building on the Cornell University campus with rifles and shotguns spurred much of the legislation. Increases in nonresident tuition were urged in a number of states. Nonstudents were barred from some campuses by legislative decree.

Some universities are attempting to counter the bad publicity of student unrest and violence with wide dissemination of information about academic and curricular achievements of students. This is done through the mass media. Some student groups voluntarily make contributions to community life by participating in worthwhile activities. This, too, should be publicized. In this manner, it is hoped that the actions of a few students will be countered with a more representative picture of the entire student population.

Students can be effective by forming public relations

committees within their own student government. They can report to the public through talks and other means on how the university is operating—and what is needed to make the institution progress.

Legislative liaison is an important adjunct of public relations, regardless of the individual charged with the responsibility. Many colleges and universities maintain constant liaison with legislators, regardless of whether they are in session or not. The chief purpose of this activity is to keep continual communication between those who make the laws and those who administer higher education.. This approach gives educational institutions an opportunity both to interpret their programs to the legislators and to answer questions that arise. The most successful legislative liaison is maintained where individuals charged with this responsibility are honest in interpreting the university and its needs—and where their word is good.

Good public relations cannot be achieved by compromising our principles with temporary alliances and political gimmicks. We must persuade our citizenry that higher education's long-term goals are vital to the well-being of their society.

All of us—the teacher, the researcher, the administrator and the student—must contribute to the task of creating in the minds of our people the true image of the university. All of us—in what we say, in what we do—are the public relations of the university.

◆◇◆ **Supplementary Readings** ◆◇◆

"Alumni, Money and Protest." *Time* Magazine, 4 July 1969.

David K. Berle. *The Process of Communication.* New York: Holt, Rinehart and Winston, Inc., 1960.

Howard R. Bowen. *On Understanding Today's Colleges and Universities.* New York: Council for Financial Aid to Education, Inc., 1969.

Mary Turner Carriel. *The Life of Jonathan Baldwin Turner.* Urbana: University of Illinois Press, 1961.

Reo, M. Christensen and Robert O. McWilliams. *Voice of the People, Readings in Public Opinion and Propaganda.* New York: McGraw-Hill Book Company, 1962.

"The College and the Community." *College Management,* June 1969.

R. Neale Copple. *Depth Reporting.* Englewood Cliffs, N.J.: Prentice-Hall, Inc., 1964.

Lyman A. Glenny. *Autonomy of Public Colleges.* New York: McGraw-Hill Book Company, 1959.

Joseph E. Gonzalez, Jr. *Legislative Response to Student Unrest and Campus Disorders, 1969.* Washington, D.C.: National Association of State Universities and Land-Grant Colleges, July 1969.

Harold W. Helfrich, Jr. *Twelve Pointers for Climate Creators.* Washington, D.C.: American College Public Relations Association, May/June 1969.

Garven Hudgins. "The Student Quake." *College and University Journal,* Spring 1969.

"Iowans Reject Student Demonstrators." *Des Moines Register*, July 1969, p. 4-T.

Robert A. Jarnagin. *Origin and Development of American Association of Agricultural College Editors.* Urbana: University of Illinois Press, 1957.

Herbert F. Lienberger. *Adoption of New Ideas and Practices.* Ames: Iowa State University Press, 1960.

"Missourians Give Views in Higher Education Poll." Report from the University of Missouri, May 1969, Columbia, Missouri.

Carroll V. Newsem. *A Television Policy for Education.* Washington, D.C.: American Council on Education, 1952.

"Public Attitudes and Public Higher Education." Washington, D.C.: National Association of State Universities and Land-Grant Colleges, June 1965.

Leroy V. Rockwell. "The Origin and Development of Educational Television at the University of Nebraska to 1961." Master's thesis, University of Nebraska, June 1961.

L. J. Stiles, *The Present State of Neglect.* Madison, Wis.: Project Public Information, November 1967.

William B. Ward. *Reporting Agriculture.* Ithaca, N.Y.: Cornell University Press, Comstock Publishing Associates, 1952.

Wisconsin Citizens View Their University. Madison: Wisconsin Research Laboratory, March 1964.

RESEARCH AND PLANNING

Harry S. Allen

◆◇◆ Writing in the *Educational Record,* Alexander W. Astin and Robert J. Panos explored the role of information in making educational decisions. They indicated that "the extent to which it is possible to anticipate the consequences of alternative decisions is a function of the availability of relevant information." [1]

Institutional research and planning attempts to meet this need. The study of institutional problems is not new. Historically, institutional self-study has been employed at least since 1701, when the president of Harvard acted as an educational consultant to the founders of Yale. The bureaucratization of institutional self-study, however, is a relatively new phenomenon and is growing at a very rapid rate. It is now a "discipline" with a self-contained literature and a professional organization. (The most recent membership count of the Association for Institutional Research is 653.) In spite of this rapid bureaucratization, or perhaps because of it, the function

---

1. Robert J. Panos and Alexander W. Astin, "On Using Systematic Information in Making Educational Decisions," *Educational Record* 48, no. 2 (Spring 1967): 174.

is still not well defined. Those professionals in the field are not sure where it is going and they are not quite certain of its appropriate orientation. The various offices, bureaus, vice presidents, and directors of institutional research differ in basic outlooks, philosophical orientation, and comprehensiveness of approach. Three major orientations summarize the variety of outlooks.

John Dale Russell, probably the father of modern institutional research, sees the function as an enterprise connected almost exclusively with the institution's daily management and its "nuts and bolts" operation. "A Bureau of Institutional Research," insists Russell, "is assigned specific responsibility for carrying on studies needed for the making of important decisions about policy and procedure and it works toward the primary goal of finding out how to save money that can be used to better advantage." [2]

Another approach to institutional research is suggested by Nevitt Sanford in his book *The American College*. Sanford believes that American higher education will be saved by "intensive, theoretically oriented, long-term studies of students and intensive, probably also long-term, studies of educational institutions." [3]

---

2. John Dale Russell, "Dollars and Costs; Some Hard Facts," in *Higher Education: Some Newer Developments*, ed. Samuel Baskin (New York: McGraw-Hill Book Company, 1965), pp. 284–303.

3. Nevitt Sanford, *The American College* (5th ed.; New York: John Wiley and Sons, 1965), p. 1013.

Another approach, and one closer to the John Dale Russell philosophy, sees the institutional research function as part of the managerial revolution in higher education. Francis E. Rourke and Glenn E. Brooks note:

> Institutional research lies at the heart of the trend toward the use of modern (management) techniques in higher education. While the nature and scope of this kind of activity has tended to elude precise definition in the past, it can be said that institutional research is a variegated form of organizational self-study designed to help colleges and universities gather an expanding range of information about their own internal operations and the effectiveness with which they are using their resources. By collecting such data, institutions hope to make informed judgments instead of guessing or relying on the intuitions of the administrator in framing decisions on university policy.[4]

Perhaps the most useful analysis of the institutional research function could be made in terms of the present condition of the university and the contributions to improving that condition which can be made by an institutional research agency.

Model Simulation

Clearly, the best contribution which institutional research is making to improved management is found

---

4. Francis E. Rourke and Glenn E. Brooks, *The Managerial Revolution in Higher Education* (Baltimore, Md.: The Johns Hopkins Press, 1966).

in model simulation. (By definition, model simulation is a device for bringing a large number of the variables in an institution together in a statistical format. Each of the variables has an effect on costs and other management matters. By changing policy assumptions used in the model, administrators can more accurately assess the results of proposed policy changes.) In this area, effort is widely diversified and major work is proceeding at a number of institutions, including the University of Toronto, the University of California at Berkeley, the University of Colorado, and the University of Nebraska. Conducted by an office of institutional research and planning, this approach can provide major assistance to both the administration's immediate management needs and its long-range planning requirements.[5] For those offices of institutional research and planning that seek to make a major impact upon management within their institutions, the concept of simulation models, and a corollary, management information systems development, offer a most useful approach.

The simulation technique is far more fruitful than the segmented approach to management analysis contained in the traditional studies of teaching loads, room

---

5. For a more complete discussion of the data systems serving both an operating and planning purpose see: Harry S. Allen, "A Single Data System for Capital Planning and Operating Analysis," in *Research on Academic Input* (Association for Institutional Research, 1966). See also: John Pfeiffer, *New Look at Education* (New York: Odyssey Press, 1968).

utilization, and credit-hour costs. A difficulty is that as the sophistication of the information increases so must the sophistication of both the administrators and regents or trustees, to say nothing of the executive and legislative branches of government. Consequently, a problem to which institutional research must address itself is synthesizing a mass of complex data for use at various levels. This problem has dogged much of the institutional research effort.

A major advantage of simulation model techniques is the opportunity to bring academic planning, fiscal planning, and physical facility planning into focus. By carefully constructing a simulation model, the institutional researcher-planner brings academic decisions directly into the planning and management process. This effort may force the academic community into making these kinds of decisions when faced with the prospect of fund allocation on the basis of systemized analysis.

But the usefulness of model building as an approach to management is also a problem for institutional research—and for the institution as well. Quantification of all of the segments of a university may lead to stratification and rigidity. There is real danger that the success of operational research may well place the principal institutional emphasis on the means of higher education rather than the ends. This is especially true as pressures build up at all levels for "greater efficiency." Trustees, coordinating boards, governors, and legislators are all deeply concerned about higher education costs. They are intrigued by the neatness of simulation models, integrated information systems, and management research. Yet, this is not to say that institutional research must not intensify its efforts in this field. There is hardly a major university or even a small college that possesses sufficient knowledge about the economics of its resource allocation.

Long-range fiscal budgeting, program budgeting in an operating sense, examination of educational alternatives, and many, many more operating problems must rely heavily on an institutional research and planning effort that develops the most careful kind of operational analysis. Simulation models represent a most useful tool in this area.

In the final analysis, however, an institutional research effort that concentrates solely on management or operational research may be less than helpful to the institution. A research and planning program that is not concerned with both the broader goals of the university and the purposes of planning will serve only to accelerate the conversion of the higher education enterprise into a more efficient "factory." Henry Dyer made this point, writing in the *Educational Record* of fall 1966:

> Operational research, uninformed by theory, goes nowhere. The answers it provides may be helpful in reaching short-term decisions, but they will be less useful than they could be as long as the questions asked and the facts gathered are not imbedded in some sort of framework, however tentative, that will give them significance beyond the demands of the moment. Operational research, almost

by definition, pays little or no attention to the fundamental purposes of an institution or to the value systems that control it.[6]

Here is identified one major dichotomy of institutional research: blending the need for "hard" management data with a need for introspection about the basic nature of the university. An institutional research and planning effort that emphasizes either approach to the exclusion of the other is not fulfilling its role.

Analyzing Institutional Goals

This article has pointed out at least one approach to the question of using institutional research and planning in the area of operations analysis: the development of a simulation model technique. In the second area of effort, analyzing the basic goals of the institution, other approaches suggest themselves. To fulfill those objectives requires some understanding of the need to proceed from "counting" to measurement as a technique. We can count the number of volumes in a library, but we also need to measure the quality of those holdings and the need to expand them. We can—and we do—count the number of dropouts, and we count and predict the number of students at given ability levels who will not graduate. We must also measure the impact of the program

6. Henry S. Dyer, "Can Institutional Research Lead to a Science of Institutions," *Educational Record* 47, no. 4 (Fall 1966).

on those who drop out to decide whether or not the mere fact of their failure should be taken as a measure of our own failure.

In a somewhat different area, it would seem that an office of institutional research and planning might be an appropriate place in which to centralize studies of how well the university is responding to the increasingly diverse needs of its students. Universities are structured primarily to respond to the "private" needs of students. We train for careers, for family stability, for personal satisfactions having to do with standard life satisfactions. An increasing number of students, however, are no longer content with "privatism," and they seek fulfillment in terms of activist participation.[7] It is this increasing multiplicity of personal goals that makes an institution of higher learning a convulsive community. There must be at least one place on the campus where the question of what the university is doing to broaden its ability can be centrally examined.

This is not to say that only in an institutional research office should this take place. Far from it. Colleges, departments, schools, and student affairs offices will also be engaged in this function. But a central place can serve as a goad. On at least one campus, the regents have called this function "the office of introspection."

---

7. A model for this kind of analysis is provided in the findings of a study commissioned by the Carnegie Foundation: Kenneth A. Feldman and Theodore M. Newcomb, *The Impact of College on Students* (San Francisco: Jossey-Bass, 1969).

The institutional research office that enters this arena will stir a hornet's nest. It would be best advised, therefore, to be carefully armed with measurement data and sufficient advance discussion and planning.

The confluence of diverse reasons for questioning the fabric of the institution has posed very serious questions that careful research can help to answer. On the one hand, we must answer the questions about cost, the extent of teaching, and the effective allocation of resources. On the other hand, we need to know why the institution should change and how this might best be accomplished. The skill with which these two sets of questions are answered may well prove crucial to continuing public acceptance of the higher education enterprise.

Measuring Institutional Impact

In the years ahead it will not be enough merely to state a set of generalized goals of the kind we put in catalogs and master plans. Institutional research must provide—or help provide—some measurement of the impact of what has already been done and some analysis of the estimated impact of what is proposed. Substantial numbers of measuring devices are available, fortunately, and almost every campus has some skill, however modest, in this area.

It is this point which raises the issue of what the office of institutional research and planning should have in terms of a staff. No office, except perhaps those as heavily funded as the Berkeley Center for Study in Higher Education, will be able to have on its own staff the whole retinue of skills in statistics, econometrics, computer science, testing, and measurement. But in virtually every university, and in many colleges as well, these skills are available within the faculty. An office of institutional research and planning must be able and willing to tap these and other specialized abilities. Above all, the office must be willing to accept involvement with the academic community, as well as the administrative bureaucracy. While functionally part of the latter, its success will depend equally upon its relationships with the former.

In the final analysis, institutional research and planning addresses itself to the wise observation of Oliver Wendell Holmes, who said, "The real thing in this world is not so much where we are standing, but the direction in which we are going." Thus, as institutional research moves forward, it must not be afraid to suggest solutions as well as to report facts. In addition to projecting the status quo, it must also raise questions. Perhaps it has been best said by Lewis Mayhew, who reminded the Association of Institutional Research in 1966 that "the greatest contribution of institutional research would be to provide a factual, empirical base upon which national, regional, state, and local policy can be based. But to do this requires workers who understand policy demand." These workers must also operate where policy is being made.

◆◇◆ **Supplementary Readings** ◆◇◆

Harry S. Allen. "A Single Data System for Capital Planning and Operating Analysis." *Research on Academic Input.* State University of New York, Cortland: Association for Institutional Research, 1965.

Clarence H. Bagley. *Design and Methodology in Institutional Research.* Washington State University, Pullman: Association for Institutional Research, 1965.

Samuel Baskin, ed. *Higher Education: Some Newer Developments.* New York: McGraw-Hill Book Company, 1965.

Kenneth A. Feldman and Theodore M. Newcomb. *The Impact of College on Students.* San Francisco: Jossey-Bass, Inc., 1969.

Cameron Fincher, ed. *Institutional Research and Academic Outcomes.* University of Georgia, Athens: Association for Institutional Research, 1968.

Christopher Jencks and David Riesman. *The Academic Revolution.* New York: Doubleday and Company, 1968.

John Pfeiffer. *New Look at Education.* New York: Odyssey Press, 1968.

Francis E. Rourke and Glenn E. Brooks. *The Managerial Revolution in Higher Education.* Baltimore: The Johns Hopkins Press, 1966.

Nevitt Sanford. *The American College.* New York: John Wiley and Sons, 1965.

THE BUDGET DIRECTOR
Glenn W. Smith

◆◇◆ THE BUDGET DIRECTOR in public colleges and universities serves as an interpreter, *patiently* and *skillfully* explaining institutional needs to state executive and legislative analysts. His explanatory function is an essential one, one that demands both pin-point accuracy and over-all knowledge of the budget documents.

Another major assignment for the budget director is that of interpreting the needs for data by the state analysts—and they are many—to his sometimes hostile colleagues on the campus. Bureaucratic forms, regardless of their merit or importance, are a source of irritation for college administrators. Thus, the budget director too often finds himself the man caught in the middle.

One must realize that the general nature of state and federal government budgeting has changed significantly in recent years. Flexibility and administrative discretion are generally things of the past; program controls are clearly in vogue. In this essay, we shall elaborate on some of these changes and on other pertinent elements of the budgetary process for higher education.

By way of introduction it seems appropriate to review briefly what budgeting is, and what it is not.

First, let us see what the budget is. It is a detailed financial plan of operations—a plan that includes a list of salaries by individual and a list of operating expenses by major category. Ordinarily these will be grouped by department or operating unit. The budget is a device to control expenditures. Stated simply, this means that each amount budgeted is entered in the accounting record. When purchases are made and people are hired, the available balance is reduced accordingly. In this way it is possible to eliminate the chances of a department's spending more than it has been allotted in the budget.

Second, the budget is not a goal, although in some sectors it may be synonymous with a goal. In many commercial, sales-oriented organizations the budget is a goal. It is also true that such organizations may influence, or at least attempt to influence, the achievement of the goal through various marketing techniques. For example, some colleges and universities advertise and actively recruit students in definite attempts to influence enrollments. Academic programs, however, preclude increases once the academic year has begun.

The budget, as a result of the previous observation, is not flexible in its operation. The relative inflexibility becomes readily apparent upon examination of the nature of operating expenditures for higher education. About 75 to 80 percent of the operating expenditures are for personnel and related benefits—commonly referred to as personal service costs. Parenthetically, it is interesting to note that this ratio of personal service costs to total costs is quite similar for state government as a whole. In higher education, faculty comprise the largest of the personnel element. It is of prime importance to retain faculties. Thus, to protect the high investment in faculty, they must be retained even when enrollments fall short of estimates. It is impractical, likewise, to recruit additional faculty at the last moment if enrollments exceed estimates. This is the principal contributing factor to the inflexibility of budgets in higher education.

Interpreting the Budget

With this background now in the budget itself, what is involved in the interpretative process?

The major development in collegiate budgeting in recent years stems from the need for interpretation. There has been a strong shift to program definitions. With these definitions have come controls by the legislature.

In Nebraska, appropriations are made by program areas such as instruction, libraries, organized research, agricultural experiment stations, and public service. Previously, a single appropriation was made for the entire institution.

Even newer is the trend to adopt the new Federal Planning-Programming-Budgeting system (PPB), introduced by former President Lyndon Baines Johnson early in 1965. It will take most colleges and universities many years to implement PPB effectively and totally. Several basic assumptions in the federal plan are invalid in a great many of our colleges and universities. According to Bulletin No. 66–3, issued by the Bureau of the Budget:

Basic concepts and design
a) The new Planning-Programming-Budgeting system is based on three concepts:

1) The existence in each agency of an analytic capability which carries out continuing in-depth analyses by permanent specialized staffs of the agency's objectives and its various programs to meet these objectives.

2) The existence of a multi-year planning and programming process which incorporates and uses an information system to present data in meaningful categories essential to the making of major decisions by agency heads and by the President.

3) The existence of a budgeting process which can take broad program decisions, translate them into more refined decisions in a budget context, and present the appropriate program and financial data for Presidential and Congressional action.

Generally, it is safe to say that these basic concepts do not exist in today's colleges and universities. Although the returns from PPB couuld be great, first a substantial investment must be made to achieve implementation of the three concepts.

It seems certain that the implementation of PPB would greatly enhance one's ability to interpret complex programs. The need for this interpretation was underscored dramatically by M. M. Chambers, of Indiana, who said: "A day of reckoning is rapidly approaching when it will be harder to catch up and compensate for years of reduction, postponement, and, in some cases, neglect." Chambers believes that public colleges and universities will be competing increasingly with other segments of higher education such as the junior colleges and private and new institutions for "scarce funds." While public higher education is competing with other sectors of higher learning for funds, the budget director is competing for the time of his institution's academic officers, deans, and department chairmen.

There can be no doubt that academic leaders in the future must spend much more time securing an adequate and thorough understanding of the types of information needed by state executive and legislative staffs. There is no substitute for total understanding of the budgetary process. To accomplish this degree of understanding, and it *must* be accomplished, a method of "understandable orientation" must be devised and programmed. Regardless of likes or dislikes of academic officers, it is imperative that they become more aware of the importance of the budget process to the immediate and long-range status and stature of not only the individual institutions, but also higher education in general.

Pleas to those in government that we are "different" no longer work; these overworked pleas fall on deaf legislative ears. Members of the academic community must realize that institutions of higher learning will be compared and measured against one another on an objective basis. The only reliable defense in this struggle for survival and betterment will prove to be a good offense. To mount an effective offense, all members of the team must be using the same signals, heading in the same general direction, motivated by the same general objectives.

A common theme is echoed in program budgeting at both the state and federal levels. This is the necessity of relating the number of dollars in a program to the purpose. It is not enough to explain that an item is "needed because we believe it is needed." All individuals vested with budgetary responsibilities will be expected to know and articulate the answers to questions such as these: Has the volume increased? What is the rate of increase? Can the volume increase be expected to continue? Have the causes of volume increase been identified? Have costs increased? Has the increase been general on all items? What is the rate of increase in costs? Are alternatives available; if so, how were the alternatives determined?

These questions may appear to be harsh to some academic leaders, but reduced appropriations or ridicule, or both, may result from failure to answer them properly. The public, through its elected representatives, cannot be expected to endure indefinitely the rising costs of higher education without "acceptable explanations." Academic leaders must realize that "acceptable" is defined by legislators as the legislators see fit.

Programs within an institution that may be different must be isolated and given maximum exposure or explanation. Without proper identification, the differences will tend to confuse other issues and work to the detriment of *both* the comparable and the noncomparable programs.

Relationship with the Academic Community

The foregoing paragraphs underscore the necessity for understanding of the budget by all parties. While some individuals question the desire of legislators to understand educational programs and objectives, there must be no question as to the willingness and ability of the academic community and the budget director to understand one another. Their lines of communication must be clear and open at all times.

Ideally, the budget director should take the initiative in the institutional learning process. To do this, he must learn as much about every department, college, and program as possible. No one can be an expert on every campus activity or program, even at a small college. But even at a large university there can be no excuse for a lack of general understanding of the full breadth of operations. This may be accomplished in a number of ways—some of which will become apparent later in the essay under the discussion of qualifications and temperament of the budget director.

The appearance of a budget as a simple compilation of financial data is deceiving; it is a gross oversimplification. As such, it is susceptible to problems inherent in any simplification. The pages of columns represent the status, in financial terms, of the institution at a given stage of its development. They represent, also in financial terms, the base for future development. The budget director, if he is to be truly effective, should know something about what is behind the financial representations.

Looking behind financial representations means more than statistical analysis and the derivation of ratios and percentages. It must be more than "a feeling." However, an educated "feeling" is certainly better than *total* reliance on objective analyses. To do this would mean falling into the same trap that we are trying to help the state analysts avoid. It should be crystal clear that analysis is inevitable and desirable. The solution is to educate both collegiate personnel and the analysts sufficiently.

Another sincerely interested group that has not been mentioned previously is the student body. The interest and concern of students in all elements of the educational process have themselves been the subject of much recent analysis. The student interest is important because of the added perspective such contact provides the budget director. Each year a growing number of students finds the budget pertinent for use in speeches, term papers, and news items. Working with students and answering their questions add important dimensions to budget work not available otherwise. Every administrator should welcome the opportunity to review the administrative processes with students; he should want to explain his programs and efforts to the students.

Current trends in student involvement would indicate that elected student representatives will some day, in some way, share in the budget preparation. This, in my opinion, is good and as it should be. Students have a great stake in the budget. Such participation will provide students with a perspective on higher education not otherwise available to them. At the same time, students can serve as a sounding board of potential public sentiment for the institutions. Our students are capable of making a significant contribution to the budget process if they are given the opportunity.

Qualifications of the Budget Director

The budget process, in many ways, appears to be one of simple mechanics. As a consequence, too many members of the academic community view the budget director as an old, stereotyped accountant, complete with a green eyeshade, high stool, and a tilt-top table. Still others view him as a link to the modern computer, passing out paper and feeding it back into the computer. These images are unfortunate and yet they have strong significance. Training in accounting and more than a casual interest in computers are of prime importance in working with the budget. Without the computer, most administrative areas would have collapsed from the increased enrollments years ago.

In addition to the personal qualities that would make him a good scout (trustworthy, loyal, helpful, friendly, and so forth), the budget director should have a temperament suited to *substantial* cyclical pressure. The pressure, in the main, results from general campus-wide interest in the outcome of the budget process—namely in the departmental allotments.

The announcement that it is time to resume the budget process brings forth loud groans. Once begun, however, the interest in swift completion seems to be unanimous. Late return of materials does not reduce the desire of an individual for prompt completion and announcement of the results.

The technical qualifications were noted earlier, but a brief elaboration seems appropriate at this point. Accounting and financial training and experience are essential to the success of a budget officer. The major or minor subject probably is not that important. However, certification and advanced degrees, or both, will prove to be increasingly important in future years. Certification typically dictates a major or advanced degree in accounting, along with public accounting experience.

The amount of knowledge stored in and used by computers will depend upon the organizational structure of the college or university, as well as its size and its stage of development in computer and budget application. It is safe to state that computer involvement in the budget preparation will increase in the future. With this trend will come increased efficiency and increased demand for more and better trained personnel in the budget area.

Our future will be limited only by human foresight— or the lack of it.

◆◇◆ **Supplementary Readings** ◆◇◆

M. M. Chambers. *Appropriations of State Tax Funds for Operating Expenses of Higher Education, 1968–69.* Washington, D.C.: National Association of State Universities and Land-Grant Colleges, 1969.

College and University Business Administration. Washington, D.C.: American Council on Education, 1968.

Harold A. Hovey. *The Planning-Programming-Budgeting Approach to Government Decision-Making.* New York: Frederick A. Praeger, 1968.

Harry D. Kerrigan. *Fund Accounting.* New York: McGraw-Hill Book Company, 1969.

Fremont J. Lyden and Ernest G. Miller, eds. *Planning Programming Budgeting: A Systems Approach to Management.* Chicago: Markham Publishing Company, 1968.

David Novich, ed. *Program Budgeting.* Cambridge: Harvard University Press, 1965.

List of Contributors

Harry S. Allen, Director of Institutional Research and Planning, University of Nebraska.

Dudley Bailey, Chairman of the Department of English, University of Nebraska, Lincoln, and Professor of English.

Gene A. Budig, Administrative Assistant to the Chancellor, University of Nebraska, and Associate Professor of Educational Administration.

John R. Davis, Dean of the College of Engineering and Architecture, University of Nebraska, Lincoln, and Professor of Agricultural Engineering.

Royce H. Knapp, Regents Professor of Education, University of Nebraska, Lincoln.

C. Peter Magrath, Dean of Faculties, University of Nebraska, Lincoln, and Professor of Political Science.

G. Robert Ross, Executive Dean of Student Affairs, University of Nebraska, Lincoln, and Professor of Educational Psychology and Measurements.

George S. Round, Director of Public Relations, University of Nebraska, Lincoln.

Glenn W. Smith, Director of Budget and Systems Planning, University of Nebraska.

Joseph Soshnik, President, University of Nebraska, Lincoln Campuses and Outstate Activities.